D1715601

THE SHAKESPEAREAN KINGS

The Shakespearean Kings

by John C. Bromley

WITH A FOREWORD BY
GUNNAR BOKLUND

COLORADO ASSOCIATED UNIVERSITY PRESS

FERNALD LIBRARY
COLBY-SAWYER COLLEGE
NEW LONDON, N. H. 03257

PR
2982
B7

Library of Congress Catalog Number 73-135287
Standard Book Number ISBN 87081-009-X
© 1971 by Colorado Associated University Press, Boulder, Colorado 80302
Printed in the United States of America. All rights reserved.

70829

IN MEMORIAM

Colonel Charles D. Bromley, A.U.S.

Contents

Foreword *by Gunnar Boklund* ix

Acknowledgments xiii

I. The Poet of Chaos 1

II. The Bitter Road from Agincourt: *1, 2, 3 Henry VI.* 7

III. Machiavel and Yorkist Knight: *Richard III* 29

IV. The Allegory of the Garden: *King John* and
Richard II 41

V. The Gardener's King: *1* and *2 Henry IV* 61

VI. The Shakespearean Bestiary: *1* and *2 Henry IV*
and *Henry V* 75

VII. The Patrician and the Prince: *Julius Caesar*
and *Hamlet* 93

VIII. Damnation and Transfiguration: *Macbeth* and
King Lear 103

IX. Parable Turned Paradox: The Garden Revisited 125

Bibliography of Sources 135

Foreword

Some indication of what John Bromley is trying to achieve in *The Shakespearean Kings* is given by the title he has chosen for his first chapter, "The Poet of Chaos." Since he is primarily concerned with Shakespeare's history plays, in which a generation of scholars and critics has seen a writer of orthodox Elizabethan opinion affirm his beliefs in a providential view of English history, such a title may cause Shakespeareans to wonder whether *The Shakespearean Kings* is not essentially an elaboration of Kott's familiar essay on the "grand mechanism." But Mr. Bromley's spiritual father is not Jan Kott but Harold Goddard, to whose *The Meaning of Shakespeare*, first published in 1951, he repeatedly pays homage, as he also does to John Palmer's somewhat earlier work on Shakespeare's political characters. In spite of his familiarity with the Elizabethan age his Shakespeare is, however, eminently our contemporary, and it has become one of his tasks to explain at length why the histories have increasingly fascinated 20th century readers while, as he puts it, "the tragedies were more congenial to the spirit of Victorian England." In doing so he emphasizes the "aura of essential futility which pervades the histories," an aura which he recognizes also in *Julius Caesar, Hamlet,* and *Macbeth,* and does not see dispelled until *King Lear.*

For Mr. Bromley is not concerned with Shakespeare's histories alone. As H. M. Richmond did a few years ago, he is writing about Shakespeare's "political plays" or, since no two critics will agree on which plays are political, on Shakespeare's political ideas as expressed in a personally selected sequence of plays. His book contains no argument why *Julius Caesar* and *Hamlet* should be included and *Troilus and Cressida* or *Coriolanus* should not; he is in pursuit of ideas which he considers particularly Shakespearean and particularly relevant to Shakespeare's modern readers, and he goes where his reading of Shakespeare's political thought will take him.

The unusual hold which this subject has on Mr. Bromley's mind is to be seen in each of the studies of which his book is made up. It is, almost inevitably, least noticeable in the chapter on the three parts of *Henry VI*, where he has to explain too much for his own comfort, but the pulse of his writing quickens when he analyzes the crucial role that he sees Richard of Gloucester playing in the pattern of Shakespeare's political thought. As his argument gathers momentum in the essay on *Richard II* and *King John,* his observations become increasingly pointed: King John before Pandulf may be every inch a king but he is also "every inch a fraud." The heart of the book is, however, to be found in the three chapters on *Richard II, Henry IV* and *Henry V,* where Mr. Bromley with unmistakable personal conviction and at times considerable asperity argues against the theory of the "seminal crime" in virtually all its ramifications, and argues for a reading of these plays which embody Shakespeare's mature thinking on "the immensely rewarding record of his countrymen's atrocious behavior toward one another." To many readers the esssay on *Julius Caesar* and *Hamlet* will seem primarily a link with what follows, for in his chapter on *Macbeth* and *King Lear* Mr. Bromley is again so obviously captivated by the significance of his subject that his development of the thematic relationship between what he calls the damnation of Macbeth and the transfiguration of Lear cannot but convince us of the extraordinary consistency of Shakespeare's thought.

In any sincerely felt and cogently argued critical work there are bound to occur appreciations to which the author must expect a number of readers to take exception, and *The Shakespearean Kings* has its share of such verdicts. It is for instance questionable whether the text supports the interpretation of Edward V and his brother as "very bad little boys indeed" (p. 37), of the Bastard as triumphant over the French invader (p. 42), or of Bolingbroke's speech to the king before Flint Castle as containing a passage of "lewd humor which breaks his hypocritical obsequiousness" (p. 66). But far more numerous are the interpretations which go to the heart of Shakespearean matters and which may, even in the very long run, add considerably to our understanding of the plays. Mr. Bromley's insistence on the foreign nature of Richmond's invasion and the basically political decision at Market Bosworth (pp. 38-40; 128-9) should serve as a reminder of Shakespeare's curiously ambiguous presentation of Richard III's last battle. His analysis of Henry IV, "the gardener's king" (p. 73), is shrewd and far-reaching and does much to establish this monarch, "Shakespeare's most complete political portrait," as the true center of the plays that bear his name. Even the readers who are shocked by the uncompromising interpretation of Henry V as the perversion of his father (pp. 72; 79ff; 130-31), with "rage and hot blood" as an integral part of his character, should be able to accept Mr. Bromley's dismissal of the attempts to view Malcolm as Shakespeare's "ideal king" (p. 109). For him it is impossible to "descend from the magnificence of Macbeth's meditations to the platitudes of Malcolm without a sense of acute loss," a reaction which is perhaps best explained by his own observation on *King Lear* that the "ideal relationship" in Shakespeare is now no longer political but personal.

And this brings me to the quality which gives to *The Shakespearean Kings* the life that it possesses. Although Mr. Bromley is willing to take on any critic with whom he disagrees, his opponents are, in the final analysis, only two. One of them does not cause him much trouble, since he has no patience with anyone who is sufficiently unversed in public affairs to accept the speeches of Henry V, Elizabeth I or Richard Nixon at their face value. But he has another opponent, not so easily dismissed, who knows the world of politics and respects official statements mainly for what they hide. It is with this unregenerate pragmatist that Mr. Bromley has his real argument, in which he admits the truth of every disillusioned reflection that Shakespeare makes on public life and views this truth, not only with the fascination of the pragmatist but with resignation and, fundamentally, also with despair. For John Bromley, the chaos of which Shakespeare is the poet is always present.

Gunnar Boklund

Acknowledgments

While I cannot hope to express either fully or sufficiently my gratitude to the many teachers and writers whose judgments have assisted me in forming my own, I must acknowledge my special debt to the insight and generous patience of Gunnar Boklund, then Lawrence C. Phipps, Professor of Humanities at the University of Denver, with whose guidance this manuscript was prepared. Gunnar Boklund's willingness to take time from his own many responsibilities, in Denver and at Uppsala, to write the Foreword doubles the debt I owe him. I am also grateful to Professor William Markward, under whose direction I wrote, in 1962, a thesis from which the present work was in part formed. While I was one of Professor Markward's graduate students, I was privileged to share the wisdom and wit of the late George Reynolds, whose comments with regard to the 1962 thesis were invaluable to me in the process of formulating the text as it now appears. For such errors in judgment as the reader may find, I am solely responsible, but without William Markward, George Reynolds and, particularly, Gunnar Boklund he may be sure he would have found many more.

It was thanks to the patience of my family, and especially to my wife Kathie, that I was able to find time to write and to revise, and to my friend John Lightburn, M.D., I owe the fact that I was able to write at all.

J. C. B.

Denver, Colorado, 1970

I ❧ The Poet of Chaos

S IR Edward Grey in August of 1914 knew that the lamps of
Europe, once put out, might never gleam again in his lifetime. Nor have the lamps gleamed in ours. Optimism,
and even reason, disappeared for one generation somewhere
between the Marne and the Meuse, and for another at Dachau
and Nuremberg. Faith in optimism and reason has fled again
from the newest of the century's generations, gripped beyond
extrication in the gap between the aspirations of the world's
peoples and their inability to implement those aspirations. The
absolute, the panacea, is gone; in its place is a dogma of
futility, of limitations, of codified despair.

We lionize the anti-hero: the Colonel of Irregulars who,
with characteristic self-hatred, became only Airman Shaw. We
relish the paradox of the American President whose idealisms
were never without irony; we mourn the dreamer more because
he was cut down in his dream, without sense or meaning. Our
heroes are anti-heroic because they were denied their achievements—or, like Lawrence, having achieved, denied achievement
itself. And science, even that science of the mind which rushed
to explore the gap between our potential and our monstrosities,
has failed us: "We must grudgingly admit that even as we
were trying to devise, with scientific determinism, a therapy for

the few, we were led to promote an ethical disease among the many."[1]

So it is fitting, and perhaps a manifestation of the spirit of our time, that it should be the readers of our century who have achieved for Shakespeare's history plays the academic maturity which scholars from Lamb to Bradley attained for the tragedies in the years before 1914.

The tragedies were more congenial to the spirit of Victorian England than they are to our own; the nineteenth-century scholar lived among unbridled optimisms which we no longer share, and the tragedies which he studied and celebrated reflect an exalted view of the human dimension which we cannot attain. We are more comfortable—certainly more at home—among the histories, a record of the fratricidal brawl conducted for nearly two centuries over a crown which in retrospect was not worth getting because not worth having. In continuity, an aura of essential futility pervades the histories; the crown, its grandeurs lost in the mists of time and the shrinking of its dimensions, appears more a curse than a prize, and the most memorable characters in the plays are a malformed, antic hunchback born with teeth and a great, gross, swollen man whose spirit is eaten by the inexorable polity which must succeed him.

Partly because of the remarkable prolixity of irony embedded in their structure, and also partly because, in point of time, the two sets of plays frequently regarded as forming historical tetralogies were written backward, the histories conform to no orthodoxy. The poet was quick to recognize success, and equally quick to repeat it. Therefore it is highly probable that *1, 2,* and *3 Henry VI* succeeded each other quickly, and then were capped off with *Richard III,* not because the poet wished to reinforce prevailing orthodoxies but because he, and his fellow writers and actors, found in their quite restricted audience an immense receptivity to the pageantry of English history. The Englishman of Shakespeare's day, living under a remarkably fragile monarchy to which the succession was permanently insecure, might

[1]Erikson, *Young Man Luther,* p. 19. (Complete bibliographical information for the sources cited is given in the Bibliography of Sources beginning on p. 135.)

take a crumb of comfort from the depiction of the War of the Roses; it was no doubt reassuring in 1594, as it is today, to reflect that perhaps one is not, after all, as badly off as one's ancestors, personally or politically. Therefore, it seems to me that Shakespeare's histories, including as they do manifold irony and paradox, were far more topical and far less didactic than modern criticism has customarily rendered them.

The histories, first of all, are neither Christian nor politically orthodox, if for no better reason than that the kings of England portrayed in them are all poor kings, although each is a poor king in a different way. That the wickedness of Richard II is not very like the wickedness of Richard III, nor John's sins very like those of Henry IV, has led some students of the plays to the conclusion that Shakespeare, out of this welter of kings, some merely weak and some vicious, sought, as had St. Thomas More earlier, an ideal polity. But the most striking common facet of Shakespeare's English kings, collectively considered, is that each is presented as an unsuccessful antidote to a prevailing anarchy. It is conceivable then, that Shakespeare's contemporaries, reeling from the excesses and eccentricities of that Tudor rule which at first glance appears absolute only because it was continuous, might leave performances of the histories feeling slightly better. It needed no Methuselah to remember the Catholic excesses under Mary and the nobles' excesses under the boy-king Edward; it is possible even to suppose that some of the great and near-great in Shakespeare's audience viewed with considerable alarm the rise of another noble—an earl, soon to be Lord Lieutenant, and shortly to be a traitor.

And the histories pandered superbly to popular taste. Foreign war—for which after the loss of Calais the English had acquired a distaste that lasted well past 1914—was vilified in them, and defense of the island kingdom, by contrast, exalted. They offered as well an indictment of the medieval Catholic church, which is permitted to stand in them with its most flagrant abuses intact, from worldly cynicism to self-serving meddling. And the sole exception, the good Bishop of Carlisle in *Richard II,* denounces the usurpation of Henry Bolingbroke in tones more reminiscent, in their rectitude, of Puritan divine than of medieval bishop.

If in the histories the Catholic church and foreign war are among Shakespeare's targets, so also is the failure in function among the nobles of all parties. While a convincing case can be made that Shakespeare, unlike his sources, was Yorkist in sympathy, even this favored family is presented in terms of a contentious duke and his two sons, one monstrously languorous and the other simply a monster, however likable. The image of the nobility which arises from the history plays is one far removed from the nobles' ancient blend of duty and privilege: to stand next to the throne by standing behind it. Shakespeare's nobles are small men, however grand their deeds and however swelling their rhetoric.

From the texts of the thirteen plays we shall consider, then, and from notoriously scant biographical information, the portrait of a poet is evoked: a man in his youth more clever than scholarly, adopting wholesale a blend of contemporary prejudices and values he very early found well received, reading the Lancastrian-oriented histories of his time with a Yorkist, country disposition—a man, in short, much like other men of his place and generation, save for the genius which was to subsume the ironies of his historical perceptions into the vision of depravity grasping hollow glory so eloquently expressed in his tragedies. And here is the essential Shakespearean paradox: no man save the Preacher in Ecclesiastes has written so acutely, and none so frequently, of the vanity of human wishes than the glover's son from Stratford who labored so mightily to go home in style.

But we err when we study the histories in isolation, for, magnificent as they are, they are steppingstones to work of such scope that the greatest of the tragedies rival, both in power and severity, the great indictments of human pretension left us by the Athenians. In England as in Athens, tragedy was in part dependent upon that kind of ethical consensus which permits—as our own time does not—the presentation of theatrical figures larger than life. If we were to gauge that ethical consensus by examination of its components, we might observe that the Athenian and the Englishman, in the two ages of tragedy, were intensely and narrowly nationalistic; that each lived in an age of such religious ferment that the necessity to believe was more primal than the question of precisely what was to be believed; and that fundamentally both the Athenian and the Englishman hoped that the social and political orders which they knew would survive them, if only because the alternatives were unthinkable.

With, then, nationalism on the edge of disaster and an uneasy religious truce to be brought from the brink to the fact of war in fewer than fifty years, the Elizabethan enjoyed—if he did not profit from—Shakespeare's lessons in past disasters. The poet did not look for the ideal king, nor did his audience, because utopias—present, past, and future—were folly for a people whose precious but narrow peace was based upon the frail life of a queen whose line was noted neither for fertility nor for temperance in longevity, if longevity was in fact achieved. As her days grew numbered, then, the sensitivities of the Elizabethans were sharpened by increasing fear of what might follow upon her death, and their greatest poet explored the past by looking into the reigns of the weak or the foolish or the vicious, and then presented to his audience a series of dramatic spectacles in which the ghosts of a ruinous past were summoned up and laid, cathartically, to rest.

The Shakespearean history, then, is the sort of play which, granted the control exerted by historical material whether factual or not, is centered more in the state's condition of survival than the individual's, and in which the resolution is of necessity more political than personal. In this sense the ethical center of the history plays is collective; that is, the resolution of the history plays involves a political solution of the problems presented, whether personal or political. Shakespearean tragedy, in contrast, offers an ethical reconstruction in personal terms, with scant regard—as in the case of Fortinbras—for satisfactory, or even convincing, solutions of the political problems. The latter, in the tragedies, are in part solved by the manner in which they are presented. *Julius Caesar* is the bridge between the history plays and the tragedies, and partakes of the nature of both.

But because it is fundamental to the study of Shakespeare to view the tragedies as the great achievement and the histories as steps to that achievement, we must view the histories as more than a separate orthodoxy. The study of the history plays is a process of distinguishing invention from historical imperative, and of distilling ethical perspectives from a tangle of political themes and motives. For civil philosophy at its highest is ethical philosophy, and we cannot grasp the full grandeur of the gestures, real and symbolic, with which Lear rejects the world until we have dealt with the smaller, more human characters in the histories who clutch so eagerly for the greatness which Lear at length disdains.

II ❧ The Bitter Road from Agincourt
1, 2, 3 *Henry VI*

THE first part of *Henry VI* is a play in which our attention is fixed upon two of the decisive moments in English history: the loss of Henry V's French conquests, and the civil war that broke out in England upon the death of Henry V and the accession of his infant son. Structurally, the loss of France is manifested in the defeat and death of Sir John Talbot. The theme of civil war is formalized upon two levels: the violent disputation between Humphrey of Gloucester and the wicked Bishop of Winchester with which the play opens, and the quarrel between Richard of York and his antagonist Somerset.

The measure of Shakespeare's artistic achievement in this play—perhaps his first[1]—lies in the degree to which the relationship between defeat in France and civil war at home is made casual, rather than coincidental; we are taught, in this first of the lessons Shakespeare drew from history and myth, that foreign adventure breeds civil war. This lesson was most

[1]The controversy with regard to the authorship of the *Henry VI* series will not be discussed here. I urge only the integrity of the text as a dramatic unit. The most entertaining comment upon the subject is Palmer's, in a note to his "Richard of Gloucester" in *Characters of Shakespeare* (p. 66): "It is impossible to decide from internal evidence who wrote these plays . . . There is, however, clear evidence that Shakespeare revised the original texts very carefully. We may assume that he liked what he kept; that he liked even more what he embellished; that what he interpolated he regarded as an improvement on the original."

pertinent to the Elizabethan gentleman, engaged as he was in
the pacification of Wales and Ireland, the defensive Spanish
War, and the repression of civil and religious dissent at home.

Reese is baffled by Henslowe's account of the presentation
of *Henry VI* ". . . at the Rose for a triumphant run of fifteen
performances in three months; we may wonder what made it so
popular."[2] Tillyard regards *1 Henry VI* as ". . . the work of
an ambitious and reflective young man who has the power to
plan but not worthily to execute something great."[3] It is obvious
that, if Henslowe's account is to be trusted, *1 Henry VI* had an
appeal in its own day that it evidently lacks in ours. That appeal
was not, as Tillyard comes near to suggesting,[4] solely vested in
Shakespeare's bawdy portrayal of St. Joan—a portrayal richly
offensive to the modern mind. Indeed, in our own time so
bland a treatment of St. Joan as George Bernard Shaw's (described by Wyndham Lewis as a play ". . . that seems written
to be played by a cast of elderly anglican curates"[5]) has called
forth the ire of the good.

Shakespeare's treatment of Joan is both savage and funny.
There are no better contrived, if few more contrived, scenes in
1 Henry VI than the one in which the witch Joan first defends
her honor and then, to save her life, claims pregnancy, descend-
ing the social scale (Charles to Alencon to Reignier) in an
attempt to name an acceptable "father." Finally, with her
naming of Reignier, she provokes Warwick to his ludicrous,
outraged, "a married man! that's most intolerable!" (V, iv.)[6]
Joan's defense, her paternity charges, and her rapid condemnation as a lustful witch are as pointed as they are unpleasant, for
they follow immediately the scene, equally coarse but more coy,
in which Suffolk seeks and gains the Lady Margaret's hand—

[2]*The Cease of Majesty,* p. 168.

[3]*Shakespeare's History Plays,* p. 163.

[4]"It is some comfort to reflect that in his contribution to *Sir Thomas
More* Shakespeare treated the alien like an ordinary human being."
(*Shakespeare's History Plays,* p. 62.)

[5]*The Lion and the Fox,* p. 64.

[6]Citations from Shakespeare in my text are to *The Complete Plays
and Poems of William Shakespeare* edited by William Allan Neilson and
Charles Jarvis Hill.

for his prince and for his pleasure. The winning of the French princess is followed by the execution of the French witch, and Margaret is no less disruptive to England's peace than Joan has been to England's armies.

The second of the great Shakespearean achievements in *1 Henry VI* is far more subtle than the portrayal of the French women, but no less effective. This is a play in which old men die and young men feud, much in the spirit of a later drama: "The day is hot, the Capulets abroad/ And, if we meet, we shall not scape a brawl." (*Romeo and Juliet*, III, i.) So it is with Somerset and Plantagenet in the Temple Garden. Their quarrel is heated, but vague in cause.

The scene (II, iv) opens with Somerset's remark that the quarrel has grown too loud inside, and with Plantagenet's bawling for judgment. Warwick pleads ignorance of the "law," but the law in question is not specified. Plantagenet, and Warwick with him, pluck white roses; Suffolk and Somerset, the red ones. Only after the plucking of the roses does the lawyer render a judgment—against Somerset. The cause is yet nameless, and will remain so. To his uncle Mortimer in the next scene Plantagenet refers to the issue only as ". . . argument upon a case/ Some words there grew 'twixt Somerset and me." (II, v.) Even in his petition to Henry VI for single combat against Vernon, Basset's reference is vague; he describes the dispute as originating in ". . . a certain question in the law/ Argued betwixt the Duke of York and him." (IV, i.) It remains only for the silly king to further the quarrel by adopting the red rose as a symbol of his impartiality among the already embroiled nobles.

Good Duke Humphrey and his protectorate to the contrary, there is no greater invocation to chaos in Shakespeare. It is a young man's quarrel—senseless, impetuous, fierce, but nominally causeless—and each of the participants except the lawyer will pay for it with his life. Here, surely, Shakespeare is the poet of immaturity, not its victim.

But the chaos of hot youth also reflects the temper of the aged. In the " 'parliament of battes' "[7] the new king (in actu-

---

[7]Fabyan, *New Chronicles of England and France,* p. 48.

ality an infant at this time) must reconcile Gloucester and Winchester, already fiercely in contention. After a brawl between the retainers of the contending duke and bishop in parliament itself—the same sort of brawl with which *Romeo and Juliet* opens—Henry attempts to kill the "viprous worm" (III, i) of dissension with most unregal weapons: "Can you, my Lord of Winchester, behold/My sighs and tears and will not once relent?" (III, i.) Sighs and tears perhaps commend the sensitivity of the child, but they will undo the king.

It is only a short step from the "parliament of battes" to Henry's abortive coronation, with which Act III, scene iv begins. Talbot pays homage and is praised, created Earl of Shrewsbury, and placed in the coronation procession. The court retires, and Vernon and Basset fight. In the next scene, the court reappears —and Henry VI is crowned in eight lines. Then, a hollow crown having been placed upon an already bowed head, treachery erupts in the person of the infamous Sir John Fastolfe, who reports Burgundy's defection. As treachery erupts, so do Basset and Vernon; in the extermity of partisan passion, they pray Henry's permission for single combat. For a moment, the king is royal:

> . . . what infamy will there arise
> When foreign princes shall be certified
> That for a toy, a thing of no regard,
> King Henry's peers and chief nobility
> Destroy'd themselves, and lost the realm of France!
>
> (IV, i.)

But only the king who created Richard Plantaganet Duke of York (III, i) could, at this critical moment, adopt the red rose as a sign of absolute impartiality. These are the acts of a temperament unfit to rule because it cannot, from among a welter of passions, select facts. And there is not, in a coronation scene which Shakespeare takes off stage to show Vernon hitting Basset, a moment in which, as Tillyard maintains, the poet "finds place for a positive example of the virtue of degree . . . a deliberate setting up of an ideal norm . . . God, the king, the peers, the captives are ranged in their degrees."⁸ In Henry's coronation, accomplished in eight lines and theatrically interrupted by a fist fight, only chaos is the norm. The roses are in place; it remains only that France be lost for the ferocious nobles and their inept monarch to fulfill Warwick's earlier prophecy:

> . . . this brawl today,
> Grown to this faction in the Temple Garden,
> Shall send between the red rose and the white
> A thousand souls to death and deadly night.
>
> (II, iv.)

The deadly boyish brawl in the Temple Garden has become a general contagion.

But it is not alone in the contagion of rebellion that we find the structural unity of what Goddard calls ". . . the play that Maurice Morgann long ago rightly described as 'that drum and trumpet thing,' *The First Part of Henry VI*."⁹ For in his figure of speech if not his intention, Morgann is right; the drums of *1 Henry VI* are funeral drums, the drums that mourn the passing of that little which was of worth in the England of Henry V.

The play opens with the funeral of the king. Talbot displays (II, ii) the body of slain Salisbury in recaptured Orleans. The passing of Edmund Mortimer inspires in his nephew York a rare tribute: "And peace, no war, befall thy departing soul!" (II, v.) Talbot requires that the burial of Bedford, defiant in disaster and meditative in his disdain of the fleeing Charles and Joan, be celebrated in the city from which, dying, he refused to be removed:

> But yet, before we go, let's not forget
> The noble Duke of Bedford late decease'd,
> But see his exequies fulfill'd in Rouen.
>
> (III, ii.)

But it is with the death of staunch, betrayed, "bought and sold Lord Talbot" (IV, iv) that this grim litany of funeral drums

⁸*Shakespeare's History Plays,* p. 151.
⁹*The Meaning of Shakespeare,* p. 28.

is completed. Deserted by captains (York and Somerset) who would rather lose France than act jointly, Talbot is snared at Bordeaux by, in Sir William Lucy's phrase, "the fraud of England, not the force of France." (IV, iv.) And, in savage reversal of the image of burial, the Bastard Dunois will instead desecrate the bodies of Talbot and his son: "Hew them to pieces, hack their bones asunder/ Whose life was England's glory, Gallia's wonder." (IV, vii.) The savage Joan permits Sir William Lucy to honor his dead, for "To keep them here/ They would but stink, and putrefy the air." (IV, vii.)

The old warriors, the conquerors of France, are dead. And while Shakespeare never permits us to forget, in the figures of Joan and Margaret, that the French war and its results were disastrous, neither does he, in this repetition of grim obsequies, let us forget the valor of the soldier fallen in defense of his king. Although Shakespeare was later to mock the martial code, never does he deny honor to the loyal soldier. But Joan and the Bastard deny all honor, even to the dead, and in so doing bring full circle the ritual images of burial which serve to intensify the puerile ugliness of domestic intrigue. Scenes of battle follow on scenes of treachery with increasing, ironic artistry. This artistry will deepen and sharpen with time, but it is already undeniably great artistry—and Shakespearean beyond dispute.

The dominant intention of *2 Henry VI* is exemplification of the man-made chaos introduced in *1 Henry VI* as the dual result of Henry V's French legacy and the contention of the nobles, begun in Temple Garden, which resulted in the desertion and defeat of Sir John Talbot. Treated as a separate structure, *2 Henry VI* is a reduction to absurdity of the functional relationships between power and royalty; the "rule" of Jack Cade is fitting preparation for the ultimately inconclusive, brutal massacre at St. Alban's. Jack Cade, the principle of anarchy, is the fulfillment of the palace scene with which the play opens—a montage of blurred, selfish, shifting treasons in which temporary battle lines are drawn.

It is fitting that William de la Pole, Marquess and soon to be Duke of Suffolk, should introduce Queen Margaret. For

Suffolk continues the image of "shadow" as opposed to "substance" first introduced by Talbot when in *1 Henry VI* (II, iii) he confronts his designing captor, the French Countess Auvergne, with the "shadow of himself"—as opposed to the "substance, sinews, arms, and strength" of his army which lies outside the castle walls. Talbot is shrewder than the French countess who would ensnare him; befuddled Henry and the adulterous Suffolk, however, are so bewitched by the inimical legacy of France —here, Margaret—that all Duke Humphrey's urging, first of a prior marriage contract (*1 Henry VI*, V, v) and then of the unprofitable, ignoble terms of the marriage, avail him nothing. What ought to be the substance of England's power is but its shadow; and the shadow of power looms so large in these plays that in *3 Henry VI* we shall be treated to the most remarkable of all the reversals in the *Henry VI* series: the spectacle of Warwick, once a captain of English armies in France, suing for an alliance by marriage at the French court.

After Margaret, Henry, and Suffolk retire, having solemnized not only the marriage but the contract which denies English access to Maine and Anjou—to both of which Humphrey of Gloucester violently objects—the shadowy alliances form. "But, though violent," writes Wilson Knight of Henry VI's nobles, "they are, in a deeper sense, all strangely passive; they are at the mercy of circumstances and their uncontrolled selves."[10] Gloucester retires in rage and Cardinal Beaufort impugns his nephew, ironically, in terms of his virtues:

> Let not his smoothing words
> Bewitch your hearts. Be wise and circumspect.
> What though the common people favor him,
> Calling him "Humphrey, the Good Duke of Gloucester,"
> Clapping their hands, and crying with loud voice,
> "Jesu maintain your royal excellence!"
> With "God preserve the good Duke Humphrey!"
>   (I, i.)

When Beaufort goes off to seek Suffolk, Buckingham is at first stung to action against Gloucester, but, reminded by Somerset

---

[10]*The Sovereign Flower*, p. 20.

of Beaufort's own failings—which are legion—Buckingham is moved to a greater ambition: "Or thou or I, Somerset, will be Protectors,/ Despite Duke Humphrey or the Cardinal." (I, i.)

Then Salisbury and Warwick ally with self-seeking York to protect Gloucester, and presumably, through Gloucester, Henry. The Nevils retire, having cemented the alliance in the nominal king's behalf which is so soon (II, ii) to be suborned by Gloucester's naming of Somerset, rather than York, as French regent. Alone, York, whose spiteful passions Exeter prophesied (*1 Henry VI*, IV, i), graphically pictures the chaos at court—ominously, in images of common life—and ends his soliloquy with a description of Henry's rule later to be manifested in the mouth of York's anarchic creature, Cade: ". . . I'll make him yield the crown,/ Whose bookish rule hath pull'd fair England down." (I, i.)

So, in a masterful scene devoted to the proliferation of confused loyalties spurred partly by fear and partly by ambition, is chaos invoked. Ribner's astute observation that "the three *Henry VI* plays, with *Richard III,* may be viewed as virtually a series of successive waves, in each of which one hero falls and another rises to replace him,"[11] is never better exemplified than here, for the wave which bears up Richard of York (and briefly his low-life counterpart, Cade) will bring down Humphrey, and, because of Humphrey, Beaufort and Suffolk.

It is in the scenes of common life—Simpcox's "miracle" and the taint of well-founded treason which Peter, through York's Armourer, brings to the Duke—that Humphrey shows both the penetrating intelligence and the rigid, instant decisiveness which contribute to his fall. Foxe has written of Gloucester: ". . . as the learning of this Prince was rare and memorable so was the discreete wisdome and singular prudence in him no lesse to be considered . . ."[12] Uncongenial indeed is the spirit of Humphrey, learned and discerning, to the age of York and Cade. Humphrey unmasks Simpcox speedily and intelligently, and commands that he and his fellows ". . . be whipp'd through every

[11]*The English History Play,* p. 103.
[12]*Actes and Monuments of Martyrs,* p. 127.

market-town, till they come to Berwick, from whence they came."
(II, i.) The repartee that follows points with savage irony to
the forthcoming revelation of Humphrey's wife's own spurious
communion with the supernatural; the Cardinal, ever malignant,
observes, "Duke Humphrey has done a miracle today," and
Suffolk replies, "True, made the lame to leap and fly away."
(II, i.) Gloucester's response to Suffolk is, typically, an extension of his reaction to the loss of Anjou and Maine: "But you
have made more miracles than I;/ You made in a day, my
lord, whole towns to fly." (II, i.)

At this point Buckingham intervenes to reveal Eleanor's
dealings in witchcraft; Gloucester, with the instant response to
even the suspicion of treason which earlier marked his prefer-
ment of Somerset to York as regent in France upon the accusation of the Armourer's apprentice, banishes his wife—making
the decree contingent not upon proof of her guilt, but upon
proof of her innocence:

> Sorry I am to hear what I have heard.
> Noble she is, but if she have forgot
> Honour and virtue, and convers'd with such
> As, like to pitch, defile nobility,
> I banish her my bed and company
> And give her as a prey to law and shame,
> That hath dishonored Gloucester's honest name.
>
> (II, i.)

We may presume that it was this same rude, uncompromising honesty which led Humphrey to order the adjudication by
battle of the complaint which, with Suffolk's prompting (I, iii),
Peter laid against York. As we have earlier noted, Gloucester's
acquiescence in the conceivable justice of the complaint against
York was the ostensible cause of the frankly treasonable compact between the Neviles and York in Act II, scene ii; moreover,
in Peter's awed invocation of the name of God, when much to
his own surprise he prevails against his drunken master (II, iii),
we sense an overtone of that credulous faith in justice which
will lead Humphrey to attainder, imprisonment, and death at
Bury St. Edmund's. To his disgraced wife he has said:

I must offend before I be attainted;
And had I twenty times so many foes,
And each of them had twenty times their power,
All these could not procure me any scath
So long as I am loyal, true, and crimeless.

(II, iv.)

But the hounds bay at his heels. The nobles, spurred by Queen Margaret (". . . whose breath ruled, and whose worde was obeyed above the kyng and his counsail . . ."[13]) and Suffolk, destroy Gloucester despite the king's pallid protestations. It is at this point—Gloucester's trial—that Henry, in all functional senses, abdicates: "My lords, what to your wisdom seemeth best/ Do or undo, as if ourself were here." (III, i.)

York is made regent in Ireland, having plotted, with Margaret, Suffolk, and Beaufort, the murder of Humphrey; in York's soliloquy (III, i) the spirit of Cade is invoked no less than is the literal fact. Upon the fruition of Cade's rising, York, now supplied liberally with troops for the suppression of Ireland (ironically, at Beaufort and Suffolk's suggestion), will return to suppress Cade and Lancaster. "For Humphrey being dead, as he shall be,/ And Henry put apart, the next for me." (III, i.)

But Gloucester's death stings even Henry to memorable wrath, and, at Warwick's urging, murder is discovered and laid at Suffolk's door. Salisbury has stirred the commons while Warwick stirs the king, and Suffolk's contemptuous upbraiding of Salisbury seals his doom:

'Tis like the commons, rude unpolish'd hinds,
Could send such message to their sovereign.
But you, my lord, were glad to be employ'd,
To show how quaint an orator you are;
But all the honour Salisbury hath won
Is, that he was the lord ambassador
Sent from a sort of tinkers to the king.

(III, ii.)

Salisbury, his "tinkers," and their king have their day; Suffolk

[13]Hall, *Union . . . of Lancastre and Yorke,* p. 125.

is banished, and Beaufort dies mumbling in his bed, a distant
forebearer of Lady Macbeth's mad agony:[14]

> Died he not in his bed? Where should he die?
> Can I make men live, whe'er they will or no?
> O, torture me no more! I will confess.
> Alive again? Then show me where he is;
> I'll give a thousand pounds to look upon him.
> He hath no eyes, the dust hath blinded them.
> Comb down his hair; look, look; it stands upright,
> Like lime-twigs set to catch my winged soul.
>
> (III, iii.)

Suffolk is slain (IV, i) by naval "tinkers"; Hall, spare of
words, recounts: ". . . he was taken upon the sea, and made
shorter by the hedde . . ."[15] The head, without the body, appears in Act IV, scene iv, ghoulishly nestled to the bosom of the
queen. The people have slain Suffolk, the murderer of their
good Duke Humphrey.

While throughout *2 Henry VI* Shakespeare has used the
people and the people's will to good effect, it is in the titanic
figure of anarchy, Jack Cade—York's "John Mortimer"—that
the people's will, spurred rather than checked by that nobility
which ought to preserve majesty from chaos, erupts with all
the brutal force of crude, illiterate extremes. Cade, not content
with being a spurious but untitled descendant of the late Earl
of March, knights himself; the Clerk of Chatham, who "can
write and read and cast account" (IV, ii), is hanged; Sir Humphrey Stafford and his brother recognize Cade's Yorkist inspiration, and Cade, in hugely ironic forecast of the political compromise with which *3 Henry VI* opens, replies: "Go to, sirrah, tell
the king from me, that, for his father's sake, Henry the Fifth,
in whose time boys went to span-counter for French crowns, I
am content he shall reign; but I'll be Protector over him."
(IV, ii.)

---

[14]This similarity is first noticed in Knight's *The Sovereign Flower*, p.
284.

[15]*Union . . . of Lancastre and Yorke,* p. 105.

The Staffords are killed; Cade enters London. "Away," Cade cries to his followers, "burn all the records of the realm. My mouth shall be the parliament of England." (IV, vii.) Lord Say, having instructed Cade that ". . . ignorance is the curse of God" (VI, vii), is killed, despite Cade's flicker of remorse. Finally, in a brilliant scene in which the rebellious multitude is alternately swayed by Clifford, Buckingham, and Cade's own rhetoric, Cade observes, "Was ever feather so lightly blown to and fro as this multitude?" (IV, viii), then slips away—to be killed, but only because of bodily weakness: "Famine and no other hath slain me." (IV, x.) His ritualistic execution is performed by the perfectly pompous Alexander Iden, Esquire.

The significance of Cade's rebellion is not alone to be found in the Yorkist inspiration to which Hall refers,[16] nor in the fact that Shakespeare ". . . lingered in horror upon the moral and social anarchy implicit in the figure of Cade, who was the Elizabethan archetype of disorder."[17] The real import of Cade is that, from his hatred of learning, which echoes York's distaste for "bookish rule" (I, i), to his indiscriminate, if once remorseful, slaughter, he is the mirror of the raging, anarchic passions of the nobles in Henry VI's England—even if his rhetoric is cast in prose and he comes from the fields of Kent rather than from the Curia Regis.

Cade is fiercely courageous, as is York, but he is politically discerning where York is not. If Cade is the agent of others, he is the spirit of their aspirations writ small. His "Sir John Mortimer" is the substance of noble claims, specious and true; he catches at the paper crown with the same anarchic savagery that is the key to the spirit of chaos here unleashed. And it is only following Cade's presumption that York's becomes, at last, direct. When Old Clifford kneels to Henry, not to Richard, York rebukes him: "We are thy sovereign, Clifford, kneel again;/ For thy mistaking so, we pardon thee." And as Warwick and Salisbury enter at the head of their army, it is Henry's turn: "Why, Warwick, hath thy knee forgot to bow?/ Old Salisbury, shame to thy silver hair . . ." (V, i.)

<hr/>

[16]*Union . . . of Lancastre and Yorke,* pp. 113–14.
[17]Reese, *The Cease of Majesty,* p. 122.

In the ensuing butchery in St. Alban's, the willingness of Somerset to be committed to prison—the ostensible object of York's return from Ireland—is nearly forgotten. The deaths of Somerset and Old Clifford serve as a fitting climax to the inconclusive battle with which *2 Henry VI* ends as it opened—a montage blurred by confused and temporary loyalties, but eloquently expressive of the mixture of hatreds by which Henry VI's England is subject to the Lords of Misrule.

In the first two parts of *Henry VI,* by clever compression and artful arrangement of events into patterns of meaning, chaos is invoked; in *3 Henry VI,* through even more severe compression coupled with expanding horizons in characterization, Shakespeare reduces those historical materials which Tillyard calls "a large and scarcely manageable residue"[18] to a taut, vivid presentation of the rule of chaos itself.

The play is structurally complicated in that it must trace the causes and results of four battles—Wakefield, Towton, Barnet, and Tewksbury—and must encompass not only the rise of two kings, Edward IV and the future Richard III, but also the death of the nominal monarch, Henry, as well as the destruction of Edward Prince of Wales, Richard Duke of York, and, not least, the kingmaker Warwick. To make of these events a cohesive dramatic unit was a monumental problem indeed, but to its solution the poet brought a gift, germinating but unripened in the first two parts, for consistent concentration upon persons rather than upon events, with the resultant freedom to generalize antagonisms by sharp focus upon representative individuals.

3 Henry VI, both individually and politically, is a duel between Richard of Gloucester and Margaret of Anjou. It is Richard who spurs York in breaking the compact of compromise formed in Act I, in terms of which Henry shall reign during life; it is Margaret, in her own and her child's name, who rages at Henry for seeking such a pitiful peace.

Henry, denied his wife's bed and table, ceases to exist, if indeed he ever existed, as a political entity when he completely mistakes the purposes of his ambitious, brutal wife: "Poor

[18]*Shakespeare's History Plays,* p. 191.

Queen! how love to me and to her son/ Hath made her break
out into terms of rage!" (I, i.) In the judgment of his nobles
Henry VI is of no account. Their references are to the queen.
After St. Alban's, York declares: "The Queen this day here
holds her parliament,/ But little thinks we shall be of her council." (I, i.) Just as Richard's eager, if mendacious

> An oath is of no moment, being not took
> Before a true and lawful magistrate
> That hath authority over him that swears.
> Henry had none, but did usurp the place.
> Then, seeing 'twas he who made you to depose,
> Your oath, my lord, is vain and frivolous.
> Therefore, to arms! (I, ii.)

is the instrument by which York is moved to action, so it is
Margaret who, against what remains of Henry's will, has brought
the Lancastrian armies and their king into the field. In fact,
Margaret has won, as Warwick recounts, the second battle at
St. Alban's while Henry was Warwick's prisoner. Clifford, before
Towton, tells Henry—none too gently—to retire: "I would your
Highness would depart the field;/ The Queen hath best success
when you are absent." (II, ii.) Henry, determined to stay, makes
one last attempt to intervene:

> K. Hen.   Have done with words, my lords, and
>   hear me speak.
> Q. Mar.   Defy them then, or else hold close
>   thy lips.
> K. Hen.   I prithee, give no limits to my tongue.
>   I am a king, and privileg'd to speak.
>   (II, iii.)

But Henry's insistence upon his prerogative is remarkable chiefly
in that he says nothing for the remainder of the scene. His
earlier double lament—for the broken compact and for York,
whose impaled head Margaret shows him—is simply a pious dis-
claimer of all responsibility:

> To see this sight, it irks my very soul.
> Withhold revenge, dear God! 'Tis not my fault,
> Nor wittingly have I infring'd my vow.
>   (II, ii.)

It is Edward who, with perception as clear as it is vicious, confronts Margaret with the bald fact of her power:

> You, that are king though he do wear the crown
> Have caused him, by new act of parliament,
> To blot me out, and put his own son in.
>   (II, ii.)

Margaret—"She-Wolf of France, but worse than wolves of France,/ Whose tongue more poisons than the adder's tooth!" (I, iv)—the adulterous Frenchwoman who cost England her gateway to Europe, the "tiger's heart wrapt in a woman's hide" (I, iv) is, in *3 Henry VI,* as much the substance of the House of Lancaster as her pallid husband is its shadow.

But it is not Margaret alone who provides the steely, feminine tone of *3 Henry VI.* The first of Edward IV's royal acts is his dalliance with Lady Grey—a dalliance that makes a traitor of Warwick, raises the Woodvilles to wholly undesirable eminence, and alienates Clarence. Edward's marriage to Lady Grey, little less a disaster than Henry's to Margaret, will at length bring armies of invasion—Edward's own, and Margaret's—into England. And, perhaps most important, the dalliance itself leads malformed Richard to "dream on sovereignty." (III, ii.)

If Margaret is the House of Lancaster, then Richard of Gloucester is the House of York. "In the play as history, Richard of York is isolated from the rival barons by his greater political know-how. But, equally important, in the play as theatrical entertainment he is isolated by his privileged relationship with the audience."[19] But Richard of York's privileged relationship with the audience is a factual one, doomed both historically and theatrically by monarchic interests. The privileged relationship which his son of Gloucester maintains with the audience, in contrast, is based not alone in self-interest but in a remarkable prolixity of motives: the new Gloucester, perverted, pathological, yet murderously regal, will, in the play that bears his name, unify the shadow and the substance of power. And this theatri-

---

[19]Brockbank, "The Frame of Disorder—*Henry VI*," p. 58.

cal intimacy is the relationship upon which the very considerable effect and importance of *3 Henry VI* are based.

Richard's soliloquy following his brother's lustful display is by no means the first soliloquy in the *Henry VI* series, but it is the first, with the notable execption of Jack Cade's penetrating and acidic asides, which has emotional engagement as well as information as its purpose. Margaret, Richard's antagonist, is as bombastic throughout as she was when showing York her handkerchief daubed in Rutland's blood. But Richard's soliloquy engages our appalled sympathy, and our interest. He is superbly theatrical—and successful. His murderous charm sets him apart from that ". . . curious demented sensuality that he [Shakespeare] is fond of attributing to military rivals,"[20] a sensuality that has marred Margaret and mars Edward. Like Lady Macbeth later, Margaret is unsexed from Suffolk's death forward; but Edward is lost in a mire of amiable sensuality, and Warwick at the French court is afflicted with a shrill pride which renders his eventual affinity for Lancaster conceivable.

Warwick is a born loser in the sense that his vanity makes him a chronic champion of the possible rather than the probable: "For who liv'd king, but I could dig his grave?/ And who durst smile when Warwick bent his brow?" (V, ii.) The kingmaker, who falls as Richard rises, is at last the least noble of Henry VI's barons. In *3 Henry VI* the kingmaker responds to challenge, but accomplishment holds nothing for him; he is for that reason the most dangerous of England's nobles. Warwick is not, as Richard is, animated by ambition; his is the most anarchic of the varieties of pride: violence fed by vanity. Warwick is the Jack Cade of the Curia Regis.

Richard is a superb military animal. He is cold, cruel, but never, like Margaret, bombastic; his pride is as twisted as his back, so that he is sardonic rather than shrill. And he is the symbolic link to the order of that other Lord Protector and Duke of Gloucester, Humphrey; with Richard's emergence there is harmony in the English cosmos—evil, but still harmony. While

[20]Lewis, *The Lion and the Fox,* p. 244.

it is true that Richard's fall is preordained by the manner of his rising, the certainty of his fall renders him more, rather than less, sympathetic. Palmer goes so far as to suggest

. . . that Richard has a virtue. In his prime he will order the kill-ing of his brother, mock at his mother's tenderness or drown her reproaches with drum and trumpet. But Richard at the start fights and schemes not for himself but for his father. . . . Love for his father is the sole token of humanity shown by Shakespeare's Richard in the whole course of his career . . . not until Richard has lost his father does he begin to invoke his bodily deformity as a thing which sets him apart from his fellows. There is nobody now to love and praise him; he is no longer the valiant 'crook-back prodigy' whose grumbling voice is dear to the creature he most admires. Henceforth he is a man apart . . .[21]

And Richard is a realist. To his father he counsels fraud— but Margaret's armies are already in the field. His brothers fill him with contempt; one is a lecher, the other a jealous traitor much in the manner of Warwick. His loyalty to his brother—"I stay not for the love of Edward, but the crown" (IV, i)—is keenly reminiscent of his father's self-serving, tem-porary adherence to Humphrey of Gloucester (*2 Henry VI*, I, i).

Richard is in fact very much like his father, but with added dimensions. The father is never more himself than when, stand-ing on Wakefield's molehill in a paper crown, he matches Mar-garet cruel barb for cruel barb—as his loss of the child Rutland will later be matched by Margaret's loss of her son at Tewks-bury. But Richard after his father's death is never himself except when he is alone; elsewhere, he dissembles. The father's solilo-quies inform, but Richard of York has no private dimensions and no goal other than the crown. Richard of Gloucester, by contrast, has many objectives and a formidable task. Edward, Henry, the Prince of Wales, Edward's sons, Clarence—all obscure his vision of the paper toy which so briefly, and with such cruelty, rested upon his father's head. But in him we sense, as historically we know, that the paper which fraudulently graced the head of the father will in its viable form crown the son—

[21]*Characters of Shakespeare*, pp. 68–69.

and then turn to paper. In the meantime, we watch the actor
act:

> Why, I can smile, and murder whiles I smile,
> And cry "Content" to that which grieves my heart,
> And wet my cheeks with artificial tears,
> And frame my face to all occasions . . .
> I can add colours to the chameleon,
> Change shapes with Proteus for advantages,
> And set the murderous Machiavel to school.
>
> (III, ii.)

And Richard, with his brothers, destroys the Prince of Wales;
he prepares the fall of Clarence, and kills Henry. Beside him,
Margaret pales to insignificance.

Henry, by this time genuinely saintly, prophesies both Richmond's future greatness (IV, vi) and Richard's fall (V, vi); but
even Henry's eloquence at Towton as he mourns a war in which
the father kills the son and the son kills his father moves us
only to admiring sympathy rather than pity. Henry defends his
justice:

> I have not stopp'd mine ears to their demands,
> Nor posted off their suits and slow delays.
> My pity hath been balm to heal their wounds,
> My mildness hath allay'd their swelling griefs,
> My mercy dri'd their water flowing tears. . . .
> Then why should they love Edward more than me?
>
> (IV, viii.)

But the justice of an on-again off-again king ruled by his wife
is no justice at all. And—lest we miss the point—Henry has
admitted the weakness of his claim (I, i) even in the act of
urging it. The murder of Henry VI is both a martyr's sacrifice
and a needed purging of the state. Like all Richard's murders
to this point, the death of Henry is a mixture of revenge, general
malice, and good sense.

But murder, however engaging, is not moral; and Richard
here as later is portrayed, as the Tudor myth of Henry VII made
him, a monster whom it is moral to destroy, and—most impor-

tant—a monster whose throne it is moral to usurp. "I am myself alone" (V, vi) is not a comforting political doctrine. But precisely because we know that Richard will be destroyed, we turn with relieved amusement to the political doctrine of the man who, alone among Richard's near relatives, he will not murder—Edward IV:

> And now what rests but that we spend the time
> With stately triumphs, mirthful comic shows,
> Such as befits the pleasure of the court?
>
> (V, vii.)

For Edward's time is as brief as his pleasure, and Gloucester has sealed his love for the king in the Judas kiss he gives his nephew.

In the three parts of *Henry VI* England reaps the whirlwind which Henry V had sown. His sowing was both literal and figurative: his heir, the child Henry VI, was fit perhaps to choir among the saints but hardly fit to rule, and the vexing and exceedingly temporary conquest of France was no less a burden to Henry VI's subjects than was the ensuing civil war, which broke out upon that very practical plane above which Henry VI both dwelt and meditated.

The real evil of the French conquest is best represented by the ease with which Shakespeare replaces the French witch Joan with the French adulteress Margaret; if we measure war by its results, and the nation by its afflictions, England bore no greater burden in the protracted agony of the fifteenth century than the legacy of Henry V. Shakespeare treats France not as an enemy but as a disease. In *3 Henry VI* the nominal monarch, having disinherited his progeny to preserve his crown, comments with bitter reason upon a bitter legacy:

> But, Clifford, tell me, didst thou ever hear
> That things ill-got had ever had success?
> And happy always was it for that son
> Whose father for his hoarding went to hell?
> I'll leave my son my virtuous deeds behind,
> And would my father had left me no more!
>
> (II, ii.)

If, as Wilson Knight suggests, "in the person of Henry V
Shakespeare attempted a blend of righteousness and power,"[22]
his son, ripened by calamity and matured in disaster, seemed not
to feel the requisite gratitude. Henry VI's legacy in fact and
in drama was a twofold curse; in his reign the ultimate calamity
of his father's overreaching abroad coincided with its inevitable,
and intertwined, consequences at home. "It is significant that
the last of the English were driven out of France in 1453 and
that the Wars of the Roses began only two years later in the
streets of St. Albans. The return of the garrisons and armies
from overseas filled England with knights and archers, accus-
tomed to war, license, and plunder and fit for any mischief.
The unemployed and starving veteran was dangerous enough,
but yet more dangerous was the 'company' of warriors in private
employment, kept together by its paymaster when the French
war was over, to further his political ambitions or his designs
upon his neighbors' estates."[23]

So, as the banner of England was lowered throughout France,
the standard of rebellion was raised at home. The son of the
beheaded Earl of Cambridge grew as the king waned and with-
ered between Lords Protector, and while we greet the rise of
York's malformed son with moral horror, we rejoice in his energy.

The real pattern of authority in any play, if two conflict, is
not that which nominally exists but that which is emotionally
real; the great testament to Shakespeare's genius at this early
date is that he fixes his attention not upon the crown, save as
a symbol, but upon the exertions of men reaching for it. Henry
is a saint, Edward a lecher, Warwick a soldier whose only real
fidelity is to his conception of self. The passage of power in
the three parts of *Henry VI* is different from the passage of the
crown. Shakespeare's most pointed irony in these plays is the
transfer, not of the fiction of the crown but of the fact of
power—from Lord Protector to Lord Protector, from Duke of
Gloucester to Duke of Gloucester.

[22]*The Sovereign Flower,* pp. 36–37.
[23]Trevelyan, *History of England,* Vol. I, pp. 338–39.

Humphrey, Duke of Gloucester, is a man whose sole flaw is honesty in an invidious time; after his murder it is with relief that we encounter Richard of Gloucester, Palmer's "engaging monster." He is not only a spur to the ambition of his mildly conscience-bound father but also the figure in whom, for purposes however evil and by means however devious, power and royalty shall be one. More than by any other single device, the three parts of *Henry VI* are given unity by the two dukes, one too good for his time and the other wicked enough to enslave its spirit.

And we must not forget the poet's scathing commentary upon the French conquest: the cities of France purged by a witch who claims to be pregnant—the witch whose place in the English commonwealth is taken upon her death by the French harlot who rends petitions.

Here, then, is the world of the three parts of *Henry VI*: a kingdom dominated by witches and dukes, flawed beyond redemption by the Lancastrian usurpation and the effects of the disastrous French conquest, a land whose child-king reigns but cannot rule, where public virtue is dead and private virtue is extinguished with the murder of the good Duke Humphrey and in the blood of Henry VI.

Tillyard suggests a moral: "In none of the plays is there a hero: and one of the reasons is that there is an unnamed protagonist dominating all four. It is England, or in Morality terms *Respublica*. . . . She is brought near ruin through not being true to herself; yielding to French witchcraft and being divided in mind. But God, though he punishes her, pities her and in the end through his grace allows the suppressed good in her to assert itself and restore her to health."[24]

Assuredly the element of the old Morality is here, although the personification is notable by its absence; no less assuredly here is the hand of Hall and Holinshed. But preeminently here is the hand of Shakespeare—bound to no dogma, enslaved by no imposed structure. And these three plays were not written to show the grace of God, if for no better reason than that the

[24]*Shakespeare's History Plays,* p. 160.

hand of God is so slow in manifesting itself. Were the Elizabethan auditors simply waiting for the hand of God, they might
have found, as Reese does, the plays flawed by "strident monoto-
ny."[25] But the audience and the poet, with a perception far
more acute because heightened by fear, were able to trace
the disastrous course of events here depicted, and the logic of
their causality, along the grim path from Agincourt to Tewksbury.

At Tewksbury, the real victor is a devil in human shape,
not the Devil who wars with God. Richard III is the devil
who, abounding in energy and of superabundant malice, purges
the House of York of all its males. His tragedy, which is also
a part of his grim fascination, is that he unwittingly purges the
House of York for the benefit of the House of Lancaster, whose
surviving heir was less plagued than his predecessors by the chaos
of noble power precisely because so few nobles were left. Henry
of Richmond returns to England as the exponent of right and
justice. Politically, he could be no more and no less. But he
does not come laureled with the borrowed wealths of Agincourt
and Harfleur; he comes, as in the old Morality he must, to
order the hell that Richard, demonic and compelling, has
wrought in replacing the chaos of Henry VI.

It is, then, down the bitter road from Agincourt that Shakespeare traces England's kings, and the rulers of his kings; where
Henry has Gloucester, Edward has Lust. But the road from
Agincourt was not, as Tillyard suggested, fashioned by God for
Respublica. It was fashioned by that Lancastrian line which
was first murderous, then overreaching, and at last simply
inept. The chaos they invoked blows full circle and becomes
the hell created by the last of the Yorkist kings.

[25]*The Cease of Majesty,* p. 167.

III ᕫ Machiavel and Yorkist Knight
Richard III

N O king of England ever came to the throne better prepared than Richard of Gloucester, for while his brother Edward reigned in London, Richard ruled at York. Exiled by taste and temperament from the Woodville court he so despised, he rose early in his brother's favor and, while by our standards still a boy, labored mightily in Edward's service. He was created Duke of Gloucester at nine, Admiral of England, Ireland, and Aquitaine at ten, commissioner for nine of the twenty-two counties at eleven, and Constable of England for life at eighteen, when he was also his brother's companion in victory.

Clearly the childhood and adolescence of the last of the Yorkist kings were as troubled as his later reign. As Chief Justice of Wales, he pacified and then pardoned the rebels of that troubled area which was later to betray him. At Barnet the Duke, "who lacked the physique to be a warrior, the experience to command an army corps, and the eloquence of a Clarence to stir the imagination of followers,"[1] led the right wing of Edward's army. Fresh from Barnet, he advanced with his royal brother to Tewksbury; in the London celebration that followed victory "the honor of heading the triumphal proces-

---

[1]Kendall, *Richard the Third*, p. 92.

sion was bestowed upon Richard, Duke of Gloucester. . . . He was not yet nineteen."[2]

But Richard's most recent and partisan biographer, Paul Kendall, convincingly contends that the métier of this fierce prince was not war but peace. The youngest of the sons of the illustrious Duke of York, and the only one of them born in England, Richard was most at home in his father's dukedom and city. Indeed, the record of the city of York's defiance of Henry VII is a testament to the greatness of Richard's rule in the north, and it was only through the treacherous exercises of the Earl of Northumberland that the men of the city of York were late upon the road rather than at Market Bosworth in 1485. While it was in the most fundamental sense Richard's defect as king to attempt to impose upon all his dominions the justice that had characterized his rule of the north, it is greatly to his credit that he tried at all. At Market Bosworth Richard was betrayed rather than defeated, and Kendall argues persuasively that the ingredients of his greatness were themselves the seeds of treachery that flowered in the presence of four armies— one Tudor, one Royal, and two Stanley, waiting to pick the winner—upon that unhappy field:

The gifts which Richard had bestowed out of generosity rather than policy, the treasure he had dispensed to show his good will when he might have withhheld it to toughen the sinews of his enterprise, the justice he had done at the risk of alienating powerful interests, the services he had performed for the weak—all these did little for him now. His kindness to the wives of rebels, his munificence to friends, his statutes to curb oppressions, his attention to the humble causes of commoners, would not stead him in the hour of mustering a steel host.[3]

Indeed, in the historical Richard before Bosworth—curiously indolent, lost in the void created by the deaths of his son and beloved wife, surrounding himself with treacherous nobles whose depths he had plumbed before—we find some of Shakespeare's Richard. But in the default at Bosworth Kendall's Rich-

[2]Kendall, pp. 103–4.
[3]Kendall, p. 390.

ard is a man worn by grief and by betrayals, from Warwick's to Buckingham's, whereas Shakespeare's Richard is a man internally destroyed by guilt, an Antic without joy, however grim. In Richard himself, both in history and in drama, we see the glorious redemption of "the last King of England to die, or fight, in battle."[4] Only, then, in the manner of his dying do modern historians, Shakespearean drama, and the mythographers who wrote Tudor history agree about Richard III.

But precisely because so much of what Shakespeare knew about Richard III—from the malicious and self-serving invention of John Rous to the repetitions of More and Hall—was drawn from the natural tendency to glorify the present by defaming the past, the student of *Richard III* needs to know more about that short-lived king than about any other.[5] For unless one accepts Tillyard's labored assumption that "in spite of the eminence of Richard's character the main business of the play is to complete the national tetralogy and to display the working out of God's plan to restore England to prosperity,"[6] one needs to deal with Richard the character as comical, evil, at last triumphant, and always paradoxical; and Shakespeare's presentation of Henry Tudor is not without irony. We regard Shakespeare's characters as dramatic constructs not of necessity related to Tillyard's dictim that "in the tremendous evolution of God's plans the accidents of character must not be obtruded."[7] For Shakespeare's *Richard III* is a play about men—and about the accidents of their characters.

Indeed, the entire notion of the tetralogy is no more helpful to the student of *Richard III* than is the inclusion—erroneous but frequent—of *Antigone* as the middle term between *Oedipus*

[4]Kendall, p. 417. I am indebted to Mr. Kendall for such of the factual details in the preceding section as are not common knowledge, and also for the conclusions I have drawn from the study of Richard's life, for they are, while not explicit, clearly implied in his text.

[5]"It is Rous who begins the tale that Richard lay sullenly in his mother's womb for two years, and was born with teeth and with hair streaming to his shoulders." (Kendall, p. 470.)

[6]*Shakespeare's History Plays,* p. 199.

[7]*Shakespeare's History Plays,* p. 201.

Rex and *Oedipus at Colonus.* If we view *Richard III* only as
necessary completion, the play must arbitrarily be relegated to
inferiority: "In its function of summing up and completing
what has gone before," wrote Tillyard, "*Richard III* inevitably
suffers as a detached unit."[8] But *Richard III* is by no means
simply a conclusion to the three parts of *Henry VI,* and while
it is true that the Duke of Gloucester indicates, in *3 Henry VI,*
that his story will be continued, the play which bears Richard's
name contains so great an enrichment of the depth and range
of the protagonist's dimensions that we have, if not a new
Richard, surely a far different one. In his own play Richard
poses problems which range from dramatic demonology to political and ethical philosophy. He is not, as he was in *3 Henry VI,*
simply a fierce extension of his father's will, molded by deformity
and grief, moved by a vaulting, if as yet ill-formed, ambition.
He is, as he promised to be, his own man—and a different man.

Even the title of Rossiter's admirable "Angel with Horns:
The Unity of *Richard III*" is an ironic commentary upon the
notion that *Richard III* merely dramatizes the fulfillment of
God's design; "for in the pattern of divine retribution on the
wicked, he [Richard] functions as an avenging angel."[9] As
Rossiter suggests, the idea of Richard as God's instrument cut-
ting a wide swath through the populace in preparation for the
Godly Knight places a most uncomfortable burden upon the
orthodox Christian reading of the play. Richard is not God's
man; no more is he the Devil's; he is, as he has told us, his
own man. The "I am myself alone" (*3 Henry VI,* V, vi) of the
misanthropic Yorkist prince is a prefiguration of the king's "I
am I" (*Richard III,* V, iii) after the apparitions at Bosworth
field, and each is the expression of absolute alienation.

It is precisely this alineation, personal and dramatic, which
sets not only *Richard III* apart from the *Henry VI* plays, but
also the protagonist apart from his own play. As Rossiter and
Middleton Murry have noted, Richard is the actor's actor; for
three acts, he sweeps all before him—and his audience, by virtue

[8]*Shakespeare's History Plays,* p. 199.
[9]Rossiter, p. 82.

of their privileged relationship, before him also.[10] No little measure of our affinity with Richard derives from the fact that his initial soliloquy places us as far from the play as it does Richard, and we delight in his antic villainy partly because it is ours. Only as Richard falters does our sympathy falter. Anticipating Iago in his privileged relationship and Macbeth in his regal horror, Richard is unique in the degree to which he is an exercise in participatory evil. God, who at one point after all reserved vengeance to himself, may not by orthodox conceptions be disposed to permit us to relish exercise of His vengeance in human hands so inhuman as Richard's.

Therefore the problem of *Richard III* is, fundamentally, a problem of critical method. If we were to postulate a structure in which Richard is Vice, Richmond the Godly Knight, the queens Nemesis, and the princes Purity, the bias upon which the Morality is based might warp the play away from its political implications altogether. Modern psychology, coupled with the remarkable degree to which Palmer renders Richard plausibly, even movingly, misanthropic in *3 Henry VI*, leaves us able only to agree that what the Elizabethans considered moral deformity was in Richard physically depicted, but while we shall attempt to render Richard's murders understandable, we shall not labor to make them forgivable. Nor can we deny that the historical Henry Tudor expunged from England a very real evil—Medievalism—although he may well have replaced that evil with a worse. And the "Tudor Myth" serves us not as an ending point, but as a beginning; we are concerned, after all, with a dramatic construct from which emerges a most unusual hero— not with a view of history, however distorted, with which Shakespeare no doubt amiably agreed.

The study of *Richard III* becomes, then, the measurement of mixtures: an ironic use of Christianity, history, and myth which owes quite as much to native wit as to the Inn-yard Morality; an astutely inverted blend of political, ethical, and psychological considerations in which guilt is at least partly a product

[10]Rossiter, p. 79. In a footnote the editor indicates that the conception of Richard as an "actor" was anticipated in Middleton Murry's *Shakespeare*.

70829

FERNALD LIBRARY
COLBY-SAWYER COLLEGE
NEW LONDON, N. H. 03257

of power rightly used; and a hero drawn in part from the Vice but developed with the full range of the poet's expanding artistry into a character whose initial confession—indeed, advocation—of purposive villainy is both richer and blacker than all the ink spent since to describe that villainy.

The Duke of Gloucester, in his powerful introduction both to himself and to his play, tells us that he is bored. His remarkable martial gifts are now superfluous; his deformity is invoked solely to evidence that he cannot, in these days of idleness, play the lover—though shortly he will play the lover with rapacious success. The Duke, sardonic and grim, tells his audience about a lazy time in which his patently superb intellect rusts unused. A great part of our initial identification with Richard is founded simply upon our self-serving unwillingness to see intellect, however evil, frustrated. We know, as Shakespeare's audience knew, that Richard will fall; but the very diabolism of Richard's introduction to us lends a most unholy fascination to his rise.

That rise is notable not only in that it is fast, but also in that it is founded upon a dramatic dualism; for when Richard is not himself—and he is totally himself only when alone with his audience—he plays his father, the Duke of York. The public Richard is a man of intense family feeling, as with Clarence; the Protector of princes and people, as he is at his brother's deathbed; or a pious and reticent noble, who, like Caesar, arranges that the people shall call him three times—but, unlike Caesar, Richard accepts. In all this he is a caricature of his father York. But the private Richard knows that the first axiom of power is the destruction of all who might impede its obtainment, and that the second axiom of power is the obliteration of all who assisted in procuring the prerogative.

It is in this blend of the illusory public incarnation of the bluff, rude, but well-meaning father with the private reality of the Machiavellian son—who, like Hotspur later, wants work—that we find the essential Richard, for Richard is precisely that blend, a union of his private and public selves.

The Duke of York's medicine for the state was rule by the sword; his son's medicine for the state is rule by the knife—a medicine not as different in kind as in degree. Richard of Gloucester is surrounded by the colossally inept. His father by contrast was surrounded by equally maladjusted peers, but the state of Henry VI was no more ill than will be the state of Edward V. Whereas the Duke of York moved, when he moved, into battle, his son the Lord Protector, blending a very real political function with a most unholy relish in the exercise of that function, steps into a political void. The Protector's—and the state's—enemy is Faction, writ large, and the Protector's three references to St. Paul, the apostate organizer, are an immensely ironic recognition that to Richard, alone of the royal dukes, duty is pleasure.

Clarence is no less duped by the public Richard than is their reigning brother, and the wooing of Anne is conducted by the public Richard as a hugely witty reduction to absurdity, in which Richard proceeds from a discussion of Henry VI's proper resting place—heaven—to his own proper resting place—in Anne's bed. "The eternal bully speaks to the everlasting trollop—and knows that he will prevail."[11] The wooing of Anne, which, like the protestations of loyalty to Clarence, is performed in purposive consciousness of the imminent death of each, serves as a fitting introduction to Richard as a party man; upon meeting the Woodvilles, whom shortly he will exterminate or render powerless, the public Richard, gruff and seemingly out of his depth, performs superbly—and positively apes his father. His pious "The world is grown so bad/ That wrens make prey where eagles dare not perch./ Since every Jack became a gentleman/ There's many a gentle person made a Jack" (I, iii) might, save for the neat irony of his phrasing, have graced the mouth of his father.

The litany of the Wars of the Roses which follows is most significant in that Richard silences Queen Margaret with power and force—simply by the use of her name. But the purpose of the scene is to provoke faction to its destruction, a provocation which makes Edward's deathbed amity even more a mockery than it was by nature. Richard, alone, begins, "I do the wrong, and first begin to brawl." (I, iv.) Richard's public function is never so well performed as here, and is remarkably clear: Richard lives in the opportunistic present, his enemies in the past. Even Clarence, instead of thinking, dreams—surely a retrospective exercise, even if prophetic. And he is murdered by the servitors, however conscience-bound, of future greatness, however brief.

The death of Edward is no less an exercise in retrospective folly than the death of Clarence. The hatreds of contending nobles are exorcised with specious piety, and Edward himself— the eternal dupe—is, like Anne, reduced to absurdity by the ultimate exercise in futility which his lament over his inability to save his brother, contrasted with his pardon of Stanley's servant, represents. Richard tells his brother that "some tardy cripple bare the countermand/ That came too lag to see him [Clarence] buried." (II, i.) But the grim cripple is never tardy, and Richard, aping his father, is at last his father's only son.

And then, Gloucester and Buckingham paying lip service to Edward's "peace," the prince Edward is to be drawn from his Woodville tutors. The scene is followed by the citizens' dark meditations:

3 Cit. Woe to the land that's govern'd by a child!

2 Cit. In him there is a hope of government,
That in his nonage, council under him,
And in his full and ripened years himself,
No doubt, shall then and till then govern well.

1 Cit. So stood the state when Henry the Sixth
Was crowned in Paris but at nine months old.
(II, iii.)

In that parallel is all the justification required for Richard's usurpation. While the hats of these citizens will not be thrown up with pleasure at Richard's accession, still they will go up— and not implausibly so, for only Richard, in this play, is fit to rule. But Richard is not fit to live.

"The murder of the princes was a necessary act of state,"[12] argues Palmer, in defense not only of maligned Richard but also of his own idea that Richard represents a universal political type. "The crime of Richard," Palmer continues, "is the secular crime of the power politician in every age and there is a sense in which every political leader is a wicked uncle who kills little children in their beds."[13] And Prince Edward dooms himself. "I want more uncles here to welcome me," he cries—Woodville uncles. "God keep me from false friends!" he exclaims, and we pity him. "But they were none," he adds, referring again to his Woodville uncles. (III, i.)

Prince Edward is, we suspect, far more than half Woodville; his saucy brother is all Woodville. Of York, Richard remarks, "He is all the mother's, from the top to toe." (III, i.) And to be a Woodville during this Protectorate is mortal. Rivers, Grey, and Vaughn are already at Pomfret; Hastings will die, as much for his misplaced rejoicing at Woodville deaths as for his connection with Mistress Shore; and the princes must die. Politically, they die as do the rest of the Woodvilles—un-lamented, by those who have heard the parallel between Edward and Henry VI. And not a few in Shakespeare's audience must have remembered the minority of another Edward and the over-mighty nobles who flourished with him. The little boys killed by their wicked uncle here seem to be very bad little boys indeed, making the murderous intentions of their uncle a ruthless but perhaps preferable alternative to their survival. Richard's decision to murder them is as directly taken when he commits them to the Tower as his decision to murder, how-ever judicially, the Woodvilles was taken at the moment of their commission to Pomfret.

Richard III, then, is the perfect union of iron will and superb intellect, complemented as well as sullied by a grim, self-directed, ironic perception that makes his conquest of the world implicit in his vision of himself. But mastery of the world is not mastery of self, and Richard—to our shock—is too moral a man to be a successful Machiavellian. His first remorse is for Clarence (I, iii), and into Richard as king there creeps that

[12]*Characters of Shakespeare,* p. 99.
[13]*Characters of Shakespeare,* p. 101.

curious paralysis of will, where indecision and ferocious activity
alternate, which is his destruction. The fire is out, and it will
flash but once again. We hear of his dreams, watch him coun-
termand orders. He is tricked by Queen Elizabeth and drowns
the curse of his mother in a flourish of trumpets. Before Bosworth, he despairs and dreams. Haunted by the apparitions,
for a moment he pities himself—and then, in what is his most
magnificent moment save his dying, denies himself even his
own pity:

> There is no creature loves me.
> And if I die no soul shall pity me.
> Nay, wherefore should they, since that I myself
> Find in myself no pity to myself?
>
> (V, iii.)

Wild, whirling words. His battle order, "let us to't pell-mell/
If not to heaven, then hand to hand to hell," (V, iii) is as
chaotic as Richmond's is pedantic, and the horse which he dies
requesting is the symbol of his reversion to type: the Knight.

When "the bloody dog is dead," (V, v) so is gallantry, and
so are all the Plantagenets. That Henry Tudor, cold and
harsh here as well as in history, soils his hands with the dog's
blood is simply a lapse of taste (as well as a lapse of verisimili-
tude) necessitated no doubt by the tender sensibilities of Henry's
reigning granddaughter. It is also, of course, a nod to Hall and
to the *True Tragedy of Richard III,* the structure of which the
poet could not break without its being painfully obvious. But
Shakespeare's portrait of Henry Tudor is far from pleasant. If
he is God's avenging angel, he is a most self-righteous, pedantic
angel indeed. He simply refers to God too many times to be
palatable as His agent.[14]

But *Richard III* is written about the Plantagenet prince,
not the Tudor, and at Market Bosworth the king, surrounded

---

[14]That the Tudor Myth was myth indeed is attested by the continuance
of the Wars of the Roses, which Henry Tudor was forced to suppress by
execution; "the names of the leading victims—Lincoln, Warwick, Suffolk,
Courtenay—mark the steps up which the Tudors clambered to the safety
of supremacy." Bindoff, p. 48.

by traitors in whose tents, in one most unregal moment, he would skulk (V, iii), is no longer himself. In some measure his soul is struck by remorse, but, far more important, his achievement has outrun his capacity to make achievement meaningful. "Richard," writes Palmer, "in acquiring the crown was seeking an outlet for the exercise of his genius. When the crown was won, his interest was abated."[15] Richard at Bosworth is as bored as was the magnificently animated Richard of the first soliloquy, but the earlier boredom was that of a man suspended between kinds of activity—or, if you will, between murders. The Richard of Market Bosworth has seen the horror at the bottom of ambition's mire, and his boredom now is that of suicidal despair. Richmond is an anticlimax, because to Richard effort was all and achievement nothing. There is nothing left for the king but to die well, and that he does magnificently.

The reign of Richard III was as meaningful as was the knightly manner of his dying. Henry VIII will be a quarter Woodville, not all Woodville; and, at last, the French influence is expunged. Margaret at her leave-taking sardonically observes, "These English woes shall make me smile in France," (VI, iv), and the ambition of Edward V's "I'll win our ancient right in France again/ Or die a soldier as I liv'd a king" (III, i) is extinguished with his life. Indeed, that ambition is a part of his death warrant. The French influence remains only in the Tudor army, which Richard describes with devastating accuracy, and the fact that Richmond conquered England with the sweepings of Breton jails—a memory here deliberately invoked— lends no grandeur to Shakespeare's portrait of Henry Tudor.

> Remember whom you are to cope withal;
> A sort of vagabonds, rascals, and runaways,
> A scum of Bretons and base lackey peasants,
> Whom their o'er cloyed country vomits forth
> To desperate ventures and assure'd destruction.
>
> (V, iii.)

We may presume that Tudor conquest by force of foreign arms was a memory that even Elizabeth did not relish. The ugly

[15]*Characters of Shakespeare,* p. 103.

reminder of the composition of Richmond's army enforced here might have been, in 1593, only reminiscent of Philip's Spanish host so barely repelled by weather and sea dogs five years before.

So if, in Richard III, Shakespeare created a horror, it was at least a totally domestic horror, for Shakespeare's Richard is as English as his Henry Tudor is foreign. And at the end, the evil ironist is assumed into the greater—and more haunting— figure of the Yorkist Knight, so greatly alone, and, at last, so like his father.

IV ❧ The Allegory
of the Garden
King John and *Richard II*

W ITH his customary perception brilliantly phrased, Palmer wrote of his political Richards that "each is the child of Narcissus: Richard, the fair rose, who calls for a mirror that he may see the brittle glory of a face that did keep ten thousand men every day under his household roof; Richard Crookback, enamoured of his own deformity, who calls on the fair sun to shine out that he may see his shadow as he passes from one piece of mischief to the next."[1] But it is not here only that Richard of Gloucester appears; for if he, like the later Richard, was Narcissus' child, so was he the Commodity's father. Bastard Faulconbridge's exultant "And I am I, howe'er I was begot" (*King John*, I, i) is restatement, but without the resultant alienation, of Gloucester's "I am myself alone." (*3 Henry VI*, V, vii.)

The Bastard is Richard III with a moral dimension. Like Richard, he is the state's servant, witty, sardonic, and gay; like Richard also, he is a superb and superbly observant realist; unlike Richard, he is neither the state itself nor privy to the state's atrocities. So in the Bastard we find neither dreams nor fears nor the last agony of "There is no creature loves me,/ And if I die no soul shall pity me"—a sentiment which, were it not followed by the brutal but accurate recognition that the king

[1]*Characters of Shakespeare*, p. 179.

who pities not himself commands no pity, might have become the second Richard. Commodity's knight, by contrast, leaves us with a jingle—loved and repeated doubtless from its origin to the Battle of Britain, but a jingle still. Richard is vanquished, the Bastard victorious; but each attempts to repel the foreign invader. Richard, his majesty crushed by the scum of Brittany's jails and their chilly, alien Tudor prince, dies, as we have suggested, the archetypical knight; the Plantagenet bastard, a knight in name as in function, triumphs over a French invader rendered yet more odious because more papal.

Richard III and *King John,* then, centering as they do in the notion of invasion resisted by the knight, have a great deal to do with each other. Faulconbridge, rather than being ". . . a link with the Prince Hal of the plays to come,"[2] is a link with the Duke of Gloucester who went before. But Faulconbridge no more shares Richard's murderous proclivities than he does Hal's lack of humor, for Faulconbridge—the wicked king's perfect servant, the mixture of imperious Plantagenet ambition with country loyalty and cunning—is not the state.[3] He is, and remains, the king's servant; while for a moment he rules, he does not reign. And like Richard III, "the Bastard . . . is not subdued to the quality of the action in which he moves.[4]

The similarities, in short, between the Bastard and Richard III seem sufficient, taken alone, to justify the assumption that *King John,* rather than *Richard II,* was the play which followed Shakespeare's depiction of the hollow Tudor glory gained on the field near Market Bosworth.[5] But it is equally important to

---

[2]Reese, *The Cease of Majesty,* p. 285.

[3]Nowhere is Tillyard's fervent orthodoxy more apparent than in his rendering of Faulconbridge's political motivations. "It was better to acquiesce in John's rule, bad though it was, hoping that God would turn the king's heart to good and knowing that the sin of sedition would merely cause God to intensify the punishment, already merited, the country was in process of enduring." *Shakespeare's History Plays,* pp. 225–26.

It seems to me that the secular nature of the Bastard's motivation may be permitted to speak for itself.

[4]Traversi, *Approach to Shakespeare,* p. 23.

[5]Reese dates *King John* as unusually late—1596—and regards it as written after *Richard II.* This judgment is contradicted by, among others, Charles Sisson, who considers the order of writing which I have followed

note that *King John* and *Richard II,* saving only the degree to which the Bastard is Richard of Gloucester off the throne and pragmatically ethical, have more in common with each other than either has with any other play. Before *King John* and *Richard II,* the history plays have presented the struggle for power as conducted between king and noble; in *Richard II* and *King John,* a vital third dimension—the church—is added in the persons of Pandulf and Carlisle. John is poisoned by monks rather than being slaughtered by his nobles, and about Richard deposed and Gaunt dying there hovers an aura of curious, if at last specious, sanctity.[6]

Each play involves itself in the most fundamental, if most lethal, of the Tudor political questions—the right of the subject to rebel—and the spectacle of Richard, heirless and deposed, provoked the reigning monarch to interrupt her last, gracious audience with her Keeper of the Records with the legendary, " 'I am Richard II, know ye not that?' "[7] Considering that Essex not only tried to be her Bolingbroke but had also, in 1594, presented his queen with supposed evidence that a physician

the more probable. For Reese's dating see *The Cease of Majesty,* p. 262; to the student of *King John* the most illuminating portion of Reese's discussion is his section on "The Troublesome Reign," pp. 264–70. Sisson's comment, "*King John* is generally accepted as dating from 1594 to 1596, and probably was written before *Richard II,*" appears in his prefatory note to the text of *King John* in his *William Shakespeare,* p. 421. Tillyard suggests (p. 217) that the text of *King John* as we have it is the revision of an earlier effort on the same subject dating from the period of the composition of *1 Henry IV.*

It seems to me most logical to suppose that *King John* was written between *Richard III* and *Richard II,* and this supposition is fully warranted by the thematic and rhetorical development. The question is complicated, as Ribner points out (*The English History Play,* p. 123), by the fact that *King John* was never registered.

[6]Palmer makes much of ". . . the sacramental tradition which for his [Shakespeare's] contemporaries was part of the legend that had grown round Richard's deposition" (p. 152). It seems to me that Shakespeare uses the sacramental tradition simply to render the king's pretensions yet more pretentious; the angels, after all, do not appear, and we can hardly make a Christ-figure of a man so ferociously reluctant to die.

[7]Neale, *Queen Elizabeth I,* p. 398.

was going to poison her, the poisoning of John was little more congenial a subject than the deposition of Richard.[8]

The structures of *King John* and *Richard II*, however, have far more in common than their mutual lack of congeniality to the biographical accidents and successful, if unorthodox, polity of the reigning queen. Both Richard and John are murderers and bad kings, and each is replaced with a better. There is an interregnum in each play, and each interregnum is guided by patriots—Faulconbridge and York—in whom self-interest and realism are happily married. While York turns his coat, Faulconbridge wins a war. The salient difference between them is the unalloyed joy with which Faulconbridge celebrates the accession of Prince Henry as opposed to York's frantic search for his boots upon the discovery of his son's treachery. Palmer quite rightly renders York as a man of judgment, loyal but not unduly so: "The politician who saves his country by turning his coat is God's most precious gift to a people which prefers change of government to a revolution."[9] Prince Henry's throne and country are saved by a knight who, like Richard III, is ever a realist, and whose humor, as before Angiers, is mixed with crude sense.

In each play there is a survival of the choric function of the wailing queens of *Richard III*. Constance is to John as Margaret was to Richard III, and the widow of Thomas of Woodstock, though she rails at the king's minister rather than the king, is no small part of the rhetorical pattern through which the minister—Gaunt—will deliver to the king a rebuke compounded of fury, guilt, and the enforced, if agreed upon, absence of his son.

So *King John* and *Richard II* are full considerations of the feudal structure. The church's bid for power is made a viable part of each play, and by both plays we are drawn into that vortex of conflicting and confused loyalties, ambitions, and

[8]Neale, pp. 348–49. Sisson's dating (see note 5 above) would, then, make the performance of *King John* contemporary with or immediately subsequent to the exposure of the unfortunate doctor's "plot" and his execution.

[9]*Characters of Shakespeare,* p. 143.

treason which rise as much from the Latinate Pandulf as from the Homiletic Carlisle, and as much from the confusions of York, rightly but uncomfortably resolved, as from Northumberland, ". . . a man to whom disloyalty is almost a matter of principle."[10] We are rescued from the vortex only by Richard's lyricsim and the Bastard's realistic, humorous crudities.

In both *Richard II* and *King John* it is made abundantly clear from the outset that the title of each king is clouded in the minds of some of their subjects by the acts through which each came to rule. Richard has had his uncle Gloucester murdered at Calais; Bolingbroke's accusation of Mowbray reaches as high as the king himself. Richard, stung, is at pains to set his accuser as far from the throne as possible: "Were he my brother, nay my Kingdom's heir/ As he is but my father's brother's son . . ." (*Richard II,* I, i.)

That Richard was guilty of this murder is an historical fact; moreover, his complicity was known to the Elizabethans from the play *Thomas of Woodstock.* This, then, is the real setting of the play *Richard II*—the murder by which Richard attained his majority and came to the throne. Richard is a guilty man, and is defied in his own court. He is also afraid. Bolingbroke, in deference to Gaunt, is banished for six years only; Mowbray, the accomplice, is banished for life. This is the act of a frightened man, and Mowbray hears his doom with considerable bitterness: "A heavy sentence, my most sovereign liege/ And all unlooked for from your Highness' mouth." (*Richard II,* I, iii.) It is hard not to feel that old Gaunt is aware of Richard's and Mowbray's guilty secret, for Richard's sudden and capricious extension of further clemency is unlike him: "Uncle, even in the glasses of thine eyes/ I see thy grieved heart. Thy sad aspect/ Hath from the number of his banished years/ Plucked four away." (*Richard II,* I, iii.)[11]

[10]Palmer, p. 146.

[11]In his preface to *Woodstock* (p. 50) Rossiter suggests that "none who read *Woodstock* can fail to observe that Gaunt in Shakespeare's play stands for the same things and against the same abuses as Thomas of Woodstock." The section of the preface devoted to the influence of the earlier play on Shakespeare's is illuminating throughout, and most particularly so where the influence of *Woodstock* upon Gaunt's charges against Richard is traced.

John, even before his decision to have Arthur murdered, is in some measure guilty of usurpation, for Arthur, child though he may be, is the rightful king. Like Richard, John does not stop at murder—and murder of the most heinous sort. In all but the most literal sense he, again like Richard, commits murder within his own family.[12] John, in his conversation with Hubert, is frightened, and he is made murderous by his fright: "Good Hubert, Hubert, Hubert, throw thine eye/ On yon young boy. I'll tell thee what my friend/ He is a very serpent in my way/ And wheresoe'er this foot of mine doth tread/ He lies before me . . . (*King John*, III, iii.) It is no flaw in John's intent that Arthur lives a little longer, through Hubert's mercy. The disguised Arthur dies in an attempt to escape, but he recognizes, as he dies, the real cause of his death: "O me, my uncle's spirit is in these stones." (*King John*, IV, iii.) John has killed Arthur by hounding him to death as surely as if he had himself pushed the boy from the walls.

In further similarity to Richard, John is defied at court by one of his own nobles, and taxed (mistakenly) by the Earl of Salisbury with Arthur's murder, which, however, John himself thinks has taken place: "It is apparent foul play, and 'tis shame/ That greatness should so grossly offer it . . ." (*King John*, IV, ii.) John, who believes himself guilty of murder, is no better able to command the loyalty of his nobles than is Richard. Treachery to subjects and the murder of a kinsman forbid loyalty to either of these monarchs.

In the first instance, neither John nor Richard is his own man. John, like Coriolanus later, is both dominated and ruined by his mother. He seems to depend upon her even for his military intelligence: "Where is my mother's ear/ That such an army could be drawn in France/ And she not hear of it?" (*King John*, IV, ii.) The depth of his grief for Queen Elinor,

[12]Palmer, in his chapter on "Richard of Gloucester," makes in a footnote an interesting comparison of the reactions of John and Richard III to the news of their nephews' deaths. "Richard when the deed is done only wants to know that his victims are dead and buried. John throws back on Hubert the moral responsibility for a crime which he dare not acknowledge . . ." *Characters of Shakespeare*, pp. 102–3.

which is nearly as mute as Macduff's, produces his most poignant moment: "My mother's dead?" (*King John,* IV, ii.)

Yet a king who is dominated by another is no king at all. John, so dominated, is no more a king than Richard, dominated by Bushy, Bagot, and Greene: "The King is not himself, but basely led/ By flatterers . . ." (*Richard II,* II, i. [Northumberland].) An evil and greedy mother is no better than an evil and greedy courtier, and dependence of the king upon either is not conducive to a well-disposed monarchy.

Perhaps it is because of this combination of guilt and undue dependence that both John and Richard, when they act independently, act so unwisely. Richard's decision to go to Ireland is the worst one he could make; it is also made in the worst possible way. His callousness toward his late uncle Gaunt is matched only by his avarice:

> The ripest fruit first falls, and so doth he.
> His time is spent, our pilgrimage must be.
> So much for that. Now for our Irish wars . . .
> And for these great affairs do ask some charge,
> Towards our assistance do we seize to us
> The plate, coin, revenues, and moveables
> Whereof our uncle Gaunt did stand possess'd.
> (*Richard II,* II, i.)

This is Richard's rashest moment. It is also his most independent. That he is neither statesmanlike nor even honest is abundantly clear. In a single stroke he deprives himself of York's allegiance and provides his exiled enemy with not only the opportunity to return to England but also an excellent excuse for doing so. Richard piles folly on folly, and compounds error with error; his last act before leaving England is among his most stupid: "And we create, in absence of ourself/ Our uncle York lord governor of England/ For he is just, and always loved us well." (*Richard II,* II ,i.)

This is an incredible thing to say of a man who has just protested the seizure of Bolingbroke's properties and dignities in the strongest terms, with a threat only barely veiled: "If you do wrongly seize Hereford's rights . . ./ You pluck a thousand dangers on your head/ You lose a thousand well-disposed hearts/ And prick my tender patience to those thoughts/ Which honour and allegiance cannot think." If York is later to be blamed for the rapidity with which he joins Bolingbroke, at least he has given fair warning.

John is no less rash, and in much the same way. His title is weak and his countrymen's allegiance uncertain. To his arrogant remark, "Our strong possession, and our right for us," his mother, ever a realist, is forced to reply, "Your strong possession much more than your right/ Or else it must go wrong with you and me." (*King John,* I, i.) John's rushing off to France while in trouble at home is no less ill-advised than Richard's expedition to Ireland; his financing as well is little more commendable: "Our abbeys and our priorities shall pay/ This expedition's charge." (*King John,* I, i.)[13]

So John and Richard, especially when acting independently, do so rashly. That they are thieves is perhaps not as fundamental as is the folly of stealing where they do. Each in his expedition takes a gamble and both fail. John, a cleverer man than Richard, has a cleverer adversary; Pandulf, the arch-fox, is old enough to know that he who wins the battle often loses the war. Pandulf knows that John, in capturing Arthur, has simply made the murder of Arthur a more pressing and more personal necessity.

Murderer, thief, rash when acting independently. Applied to a king, these terms indicate a man whose nature has made him a national disaster. We know that Richard and John impugned the honor of the crown; we must look more carefully to see that they have placed limits around the royal prerogative more binding even than the consequences of personal evil made necessary.

In his essay on *King John* Goddard has pointed out that "Shakespeare has often been criticized for omitting all reference in this play to what historians and political scientists consider

[13]This passage is, I think, sufficient to answer Reese's notion that John's poisoning by a monk is "sudden and surprising." (*The Cease of Majesty,* p. 275.)

the main event of John's reign: the granting of Magna Carta."[14] Yet Shakespeare has not forgotten to point out, in the person of Salisbury, the disdain which John's nobles very heartily feel for him: "The King hath dispossessed himself of us./ We will not line his thin bestained cloak/ With our pure honours; nor attend the foot/ That leaves the print of blood where'er it walks." (*King John,* IV, iii.) Shakespeare has chosen to turn his attention toward what could not help being the salient feature of the reign of King John: his betrayal of his crown. John's sins are numbered and written in the brief passage which opens the fifth act:

K. JOHN: Thus have I yielded up into your hand
          The circle of my glory.

PAND: Take again
          From this my hand, as holding of the Pope
          Your sovereign greatness and authority.

John is not to wear even this borrowed crown much longer, for, as he reminds Pandulf, ". . . the present time is so sick,/ That present medicine must be ministered,/ Or overthrow incurable ensues." These are prophetic words, for the poison that is soon to be administered to John is the only medicine which can cure the state.

John is, however, no longer king: he is a vassal of the Pope, and shortly, in a very real sense, to be even less than that, for John, like Richard, proves his ineptitude as king by abdication. The Bastard becomes king when John wearily tells him, "Have thou the ordering of this present time," (V, i) and Faulconbridge, long since Sir Richard Plantagenet, exercises his royal prerogative in words which would have graced the tongue of his dead father: "Now hear our English King,/ For thus his royalty doth speak in me." (V, ii.) In battle, John leaves the field; his presence there is unnecessary, for he is not England's king but the Pope's vassal, and he has, in addition, abdicated the rights and duties of the Plantagenet kings to another, and better, Plantagenet.

[14]*The Meaning of Shakespeare,* pp. 146–47.

Easily found in *Richard II* are similar voices urging the doom of a king who is no longer king. To Gaunt, Richard's dying adviser, we can assign the choric role regardless of his own sins. Certainly Gaunt has reason enough to hate Richard, who has deprived him of his son, but we cannot deny that Gaunt, who is aware of all the weaknesses of England's king, loves England. His lyric description of England is frequently quoted—perhaps too frequently, for the speech is in reality a harsh comparison. England's potential greatness is contrasted with bitter reality, her past kings with the vain and arrogant fop who now rules:

> This royal throne of kings, . . .
> This blessed plot, . . .
>   . . . this teeming womb of royal kings,
> Fear'd by their breed, and famous by their
>   birth, . . .
> Is now leased out—I die pronouncing it—
> Like to a tenement or pelting farm.
> England . . .
>   . . . is now bound in with shame,
> With inky blots, and rotten parchment bonds.
> That England that was wont to conquer others,
> Hath made a shameful conquest of itself.
>   (*Richard II,* II, i.)

Here is Richard's sin as king—the leasing of the kingdom to maintain, not his royalty, but his royal state. It is king, not kingdom, that Richard sees later in his mirror: "Was this face, the face/ That every day, under his household roof,/ Did keep ten thousand men?" (IV, i.) And it was the king, not the kingdom, to whom he was devoted. Like John, he lost the kingdom by maintaining the king. When we strip Gaunt's speech on England and her king of its eloquently patriotic description, we have left only a scathing indictment, and no less accurate than his accusation is Gaunt's prophecy of Richard's end: "He tires betimes that spurs too fast betimes;/ With eager feeding food doth choke the feeder." (II, ii.) Richard's kingdom has been leased out to his nobles no less surely than John's to the Pope, and neither is more than king of a shadow.

Too, Richard, like John, resigns his crown. John, when alone, has said, "Did not the prophet/ Say, that before Ascension Day at noon,/ My crown I should give off? Even so I have./ I did suppose that it should be on constraint,/ But, heaven be thanked, it is but voluntary." (*King John,* V, i.) And York may say to Richard, when he is summoned to Bolingbroke, that he comes, "To do that office of thine own good will/ Which tired majesty did make thee offer,/ The resignation of thy state and crown/ To Henry Bolingbroke." (*Richard II,* IV, i.) Apt indeed is "tired majesty" to describe a man so fitted to act the part of king but so unable to fulfill its proper functions. Richard was proud of majesty, but the king must be more than the ceremony with which he is surrounded.

"Landlord of England art thou now, not king . . ." says dying Gaunt to Richard. (*Richard II,* II, i.) In Richard's time, majesty had fled the realm, for Richard was not king. Sir Richard Plantagenet recognizes this same bitter truth as he watches Hubert bear away the body of dead Arthur:

> How easy dost thou take all England up!
> From forth this morsel of dead royalty,
> The life, the right, and truth of all this realm
> Is fled to heaven; and England now is left
> To tug and scamble, and to part by the teeth
> The unowed interest of proud-swelling state.
> (*King John,* IV, iii.)

So Shakespeare's England, in the time of Richard and in the time of John, is a kingdom without a king; and the difference between Gaunt's ideal England and the real England is a measure of the ineptitude and depravity of the kings. The land is sick and needs strong medicine. In *King John* the medicine is the king's death and the accession of Prince Henry; in *Richard II* chaos and misrule will shortly be succeeded by the iron rule of Henry Bolingbroke.

In a cataloguing of comparable sins, then, John and Richard are much alike. They are bad men; they are bad kings; and they are both thoroughly frightened. When John, upon his return from France, is crowned again, he puts off Salisbury's and Pem-

broke's questionings of this procedure in words made evasive
by terror: "Some reasons of this double coronation/ I have possessed you with, and think them strong;/ And more, more strong,
the lesser is my fear,/ I shall indue you with." (*King John,* IV,
ii.) Only a man stricken with terror could view Arthur as a
"serpent." (*King John,* III, iii.) Richard, returned from Ireland, is no less frightened; the Bishop of Carlisle has need to
reassure him: "Fear not my lord, the Power that made you
King,/ Hath power to keep you King in spite of all." (*Richard
II,* III, ii.)

Richard and John alike resort to the sheerest hypocrisy to
wash away both guilt and fear. Hamlet's "Words! Words!
Words!" and the Bastard's comment upon the royal parley before Angiers, "Zounds, I was never so bethumped with words,/
Since I first called my brother's father dad" (*King John,* II, i),
will stand as Shakespeare's comment upon users of excess verb-
iage. Talking too much, with too little sincerity and meaning,
is Richard's besetting sin, and, to a lesser extent, John's also.

Certainly Richard is an able rhetorician, but his many fine
words serve most often to reveal his empty concept of kingship.
Despairingly he describes the crown as "hollow," and in the
same moment he speaks of equality he sets himself apart
from all that equality demands: ". . . throw away respect,/
Tradition, form, and ceremonious duty,/ For you have but
mistook me all this while./ I live with bread like you, feel want,/
Taste grief, need friends; subjected thus,/ How can you say to
me I am a King?" (*Richard II,* III, ii.)

"Respect," "tradition," "form," and "ceremonious duty"—
these are the terms that describe Richard's feelings of what
a king is. It is about ceremonious duty that he addresses Northumberland: "We are amazed, and thus long have we stood,/
To watch the fearful bending of thy knee,/ Because we thought
ourself thy lawful King./ And if we be, how dare thy joints for-
get/ To pay their awful duty to our presence?" (III, iii.) And
when Richard descends to the "Base court where kings grow
base,/ To come at traitors' calls, and do them grace," he speaks
to Bolingbroke too upon the subject of ceremonious duty, al-

though ironically: "Fair cousin, you debase your princely knee,/ To make the base earth proud with kissing it." (III, iii.)

But nowhere does Richard better illustrate the extent to which he equates ceremony with kingship than at the moment when he enters Westminster Hall: "I hardly yet have learned/ To insinuate, flatter, bow, and bend my knee." (IV, i.) Here in two lines is Richard's concept of kingship. So he was treated when he was king, and now, filled with bitterness and false humility, it is in these terms that he rages at his tormentors. The "mockery king of snow" richly deserves Bolingbroke's devastating "The shadow of your sorrow hath destroyed/ The shadow of your face." (IV, i.)

Richard plays with words so much that he plays the crown right off his head, but he has meant to do it. To Bolingbroke at Flint Castle he has flippantly but purposively remarked:

> Cousin I am too young to be your father
> Though you are old enough to be my heir.
> What you will have, I'll give, and willing too,
> For do we must, what force will have us do.
> Set on towards London, cousin, is it so?
>
> (III ,iii.)

There speaks the real, the essential, Richard. He hides beneath a mask of words. He wishes to reign, but not to be king; he is forced off his throne, but he meets the superior force of Bolingbroke eagerly. He embraces it, as a child might welcome a storm. "Now, mark me how I will undo myself/I give this heavy weight from off my head,/ And this unwieldly sceptre from my hand . . ." (IV, i.)

Here, as Richard deposes himself, he is superb. He is also eager, frantically eager. To the queen's question, "What, is my Richard both in shape and mind/ Transformed and weakened? Hath Bolingbroke deposed/ Thine intellect?" (V, i) he might reply that his intellect, like his throne, has been weakened and lost by his own, not Bolingbroke's, hand. Richard surrenders the crown in characteristically graceful, measured, if self-pitying words; it is not until he is asked to read "These accusations,

and these grievous crimes,/ Committed by your person, and
your followers,/ Against the state and profit of this land . . ."
that the savagery which so mars his death breaks through the
genuine majesty of his resignation of the crown. Conscious of
his guilt, and made frantic by this consciousness, he pours forth
denials and accusations, prefaced by a pitiful and genuine
confession: "Must I do so? And must I ravel out/ My weaved-
up follies?" Earlier in the same scene, Richard in his omni-
present vanity has drawn an ill-considered parallel: "Yet well
I remember/ The favours of these men: were they not mine?/
Did they not sometime cry all hail to me?/ So Judas did to
Christ: but he in twelve,/ Found truth in all, but one; I, in
twelve thousand,/ none." (IV, i.)

That is no more than an addition to Richard's earlier view
of the source of his deliverance: "For every man that Bolingbroke hath pressed,/ To lift shrewd steel against our golden
crown,/ God for his Richard hath in heavenly pay/ A glorious
angel . . ." (III, ii.) There appear two flagrant errors, each
showing the extent to which Richard's mind has strayed from
reality. First, neither Richard nor any man like him could be
God's in the sense Richard intends; second, to combat a king
like Richard, Bolingbroke did not have to resort to impress-
ment. Richard here is maddened by the sound of his own voice,
as he is later by the music at Pomfret, and madness piled upon
madness becomes grandly expressed idiocy: "Yet know, my
master God omnipotent,/ Is mustering in his clouds on our
behalf,/ Armies of pestilence, and they shall strike/ Your children yet unborn, and unbegot,/ That lift your vassal hands
against my head . . ." (III, iii.) To this threat and others like
it, Shakespeare provides a reply pitiful to the same degree that
the threats have been grandiose.

> K. Rich. God save the King! Will no man say, amen?
> Am I both priest, and clerk? Well then, amen.
>
>   (IV, i.)

John, a more simply drawn character than Richard, is a
man whose words are made mockery by his actions. Not even
John of Gaunt expresses more fervent patriotism than does King

John in his defiant reply to Pandulf upon the question of Lang-
ton's installation as archbishop:

> What earthly name to interrogatories
> Can task the free breath of a sacred King?
> Thou canst not, Cardinal, devise a name
> So slight, unworthy, and ridiculous,
> To charge me to an answer, as the Pope.
> Tell him this tale; and from the mouth of England,
> Add thus much more, that no Italian priest
> Shall tithe or toll in our dominions.
> But as we, under Heaven, are supreme head,
> So under Him that great supremacy
> Where we do reign, we will alone uphold
> Without the assistance of a mortal hand.
>   (*King John*, III, i.)

There is the heart of the Reformation in England. "Supreme
head" is the expression Henry VIII used, and these words of
John's are the essence of the Tudor religion, quite in the spirit
of the lengthy pre-Tudor resistance to the papacy. Here John,
like Richard on the wall at Flint Castle, is every inch a king.
He is also every inch a fraud. Where Richard II is entranced
by words, John is, as was Richard III, captivated by the possi-
bility of manipulating the events and personages around him.
He is a complete opportunist—the epitome of Commodity. His
lines to Hubert, "How oft the sight of means to do ill deeds/
Make ill deeds done" (*King John*, IV, ii), represent a sentiment
worthy of Iago, the supreme manipulator. This is as close as
we can come to the essential John, who seems a worse man
than Richard only because Richard's evil is more magnificently
hidden. Richard is given great rhetoric; John is given only lies.

Neither of these two kings dies better than he has lived.
Prince Henry's description of John's tranquility is belied by
John's own "Within me is a hell . . ." (*King John*, V, vii.)
There is no personal peace in the death of John, and he is not
even granted the cold comfort of knowing that political peace
has been concluded. Indeed, Prince Henry has inherited a sorry
mess, which Salisbury, whose tongue is as quick as his loyalties,
describes with exactitude as he comforts Henry: "Be of good

comfort Prince, for you are born/ To set a form upon that
indigest/ Which he hath left so shapeless and so rude." (*King
John,* V, vii.) The "hell" within John is matched by the
hellish chaos which is his legacy to his son.

Richard, like John, sings before his death; "as a performer
on the lyre Richard has no match among Shakespeare's many
people. And as dramatizer of himself he will be tutor to a
long posterity."[15] Richard rhapsodizes upon the subject of his
death before the event, in the sweet and pathetic tones which
are his singular gift:

> Good sometimes Queen, prepare thee hence for France.
> Think I am dead, and that even here thou tak'st,
> As from my death-bed, thy last living leave.
> In winter's tedious nights sit by the fire,
> With good old folks and let them tell thee tales
> Of woeful ages long ago betid;
> And ere thou bid good night, to quite their griefs,
> Tell thou the lamentable tale of me,
> And send the hearers weeping to their beds.
>
> (V, i.)

It is a moving speech—so moving that the senseless cruelty of
this injunction to a genuinely grieving wife is overlooked. It
might be forgivable if Richard were honestly trying to comfort
the queen, but he is really attempting only to alleviate his own
fear and self-pity by rehearsing, and relishing, the effects of the
end which he himself has so eagerly sought. "The thought of
his own death is delicious pleasure; the alliteration in the third
line is something of which he is conscious and sadly proud; the
good old folks in France are already weeping for him as he
sings."[16]

In Pomfret Castle, Richard tries to play a new, and his
penultimate, role—that of philosopher. And at times in his soliloquy, he comes near to the truth of an existence that has touched
reality only where it touched contrast and comparison. He has
acted many roles, but he has never reached, and does not here

[15]Van Doren, p. 78.
[16]Van Doren, p. 77.

attain, any concrete level of reality in his own nature. He does achieve a measure of self-realization comparable to John's "Within me is a hell" when he muses, "Thus play I in one person many people/ And none contented . . ." and again, "I wasted time, and now doth time waste me." (*Richard II, V, v.*) Yet in the same scene he can command, when his keeper brings him food, "Taste of it first as thou art wont to do." A true philosopher would hardly bother to request the services of a taster when he knew that death in some form was imminent. Richard is no more philosopher than he was king.[17]

In his last, and worst, role—that of the man of action— Richard violently attacks his keeper, and, when he has been stabbed by the assassins, reverts to the wild, vain threats with which he had sought to support his pretense of royalty. He is perhaps attempting to fulfill his queen's mildly scornful portrait of gallant death: "The lion dying thrusteth forth his paw,/ And wounds the earth, if nothing else, with rage,/ To be o'erpowered . . ." (*Richard II, V, i.*) But Richard does not succeed and is not convincing. Exton's eulogy, "As full of valour as of royal blood," (*Richard II, V, v*) is nothing more than a fool's commentary upon another fool.

Strangely, Richard's ultimate act has often been admird as bravery, a final burst of courage from a coward. It is nothing of the sort. We die as we have lived. It is just the reflex action of a man without self-control in the presence of death, as little willed as the galvanic twitching of a frog's leg. It is a fury of desperation pure and simple, a particularly ignominious and ironic end for a king who pretended to believe that everything from stones to angels would come to his rescue in the hour of need.[18]

The greatest of the many ironies of *Richard III, King John,* and *Richard II*—and their most frequently overlooked common

[17]It seems to me that Wilson Knight's treatment of Richard's soliloquy as a pattern from which emerges Shakespeare's mind and art is overstated. For instance: "So Richard, in poetic mood, becomes a true poet, a miniature of the future Shakespeare, his thought turning on that very axis about which the visionary sequence of plays unwritten was destined to revolve." (*The Imperial Theme,* p. 362.)

[18]Goddard, p. 159.

feature—is that each ends with a note of perfection that is purely nominal.

If one were able to ignore the fact that Henry Tudor's harsh rule provoked rebellion by imposture because legitimacy was dead or imprisoned, one might conclude with Tillyard that Henry brought the dawn of a new day rather than merely a grim perpetuation of the old. The dramatic tension at the end of *Richard III* is generated, not by the conqueror, but by the splendid medievalism of the king's dying. The ending of *King John,* however nominally prophetic of perfection to come, cleverly underscores the youth and inexperience of the prince by giving the last speech to the character of least noble origin. And the polity of Henry IV is no less nominally flawless; Bolingbroke succeeds precisely where Richard most signally failed.[19] The pious banishment of Sir Pierce of Exton, reminiscent though it may be of Richard III's murders and the method of John's death, is rendered more rather than less politically plausible by the grim, pastoral imagery in which it is couched: "Lords, I protest my soul is full of woe/ That blood should sprinkle me to make me grow." (*Richard II,* V, vi.) The metaphor of the king's being a plant nourished by the blood of his predecessor is appropriate for a monarch who, perhaps like John's monks, loved not the poison that he needed.

All three of these plays, then, end in truce rather than peace, and while the story of only one monarch, Henry IV, is to be continued, the three plays are similar in that each depicts a king flawed beyond redemption who is replaced with a successor either good or strong beyond plausibility. Also, the three share a common political problem: the relationship which must be imposed, because it cannot be agreed upon or negotiated, between the sovereign and his subjects.

It was in dealing with Richard III that Shakespeare began to consider the right exercise of power a futile exercise, since the crown destroys even the demonic. Faulconbridge is rescued

[19]Palmer notes the fact that Richard's most demonstrable weakness—the inability to immobilize noble feuds—is Bolingbroke's strength. (*Characters of Shakespeare,* p. 160.)

because the royalty which exalts—or taints—his blood does not grace his brow, and his king, the tactician without art, is devoured by a poison more internally generated than externally applied. Even the last lyrics of the poet, Richard II, are flawed by that same easy, deadly self-pity by which he talked his crown off his head; in Pomfret Castle he commands that the music be stopped so that his exhausted majesty may hear only itself.

But, writes Reese, "Shakespeare's quest in the histories was not only the ideal king, since even the most dedicated ruler must fail when his subjects are corrupt; he was also seeking the ideal social relationship in which king and people were united in a conception of their mutual duty."[20] We would hesitate to describe Shakespeare's purpose in the history plays as the search for an ideal ruler, since to this point, from foolish Henry VI to the stunted Narcissus Richard II, Shakespeare has selected from among the vast materials available to him only the reigns of disastrous kings—which are, after all, far better theater than the reigns of good kings.

But the "ideal social relationship" which Reese rightly regards as that condition of political life upon which an ideal polity must be founded is detailed, and very carefully detailed, in the Garden Scene in *Richard II*. The Allegory of the Garden there—intrusive, doctrinal, and, to the modern mind, unpleasant—describes precisely the relationship that must obtain between the governor and the governed:

> Go, bind thou up yon dangling apricocks,
> Which, like unruly children, make their sire
> Stoop with oppression of their prodigal weight;
> Give some supportance to the bending twigs.
> Go thou, and like an executioner,
> Cut off the heads of too fast-growing sprays,
> That look too lofty in our commonwealth;
> All must be even in our government.
> (*Richard II*, III, iv.)[21]

[20]*The Cease of Majesty*, p. vii.

[21]Palmer (p. 168), here devoid of his usual acute political sensitivity, treats the allegory as little more than a pastoral prelude to the meeting of king and queen. Goddard, to whose essay on *Richard II* the Garden

Lest the audience for "old Adam's likeness" mistake his point, the gardener relates his parable directly to the action of the play. To bind, then, is to imprison; to execute is simply to ensure that no man's head stands higher than the king's. And the reason for this doctrinal allegory is clear; the poet, no less provoked than other men to reflect upon the gap—however moralized in his sources—between the desirable and the real, has traced a series of royal disasters which only suppression and confiscation might have stopped. And the Wars of the Roses in point of fact bear no little resemblance to the weeding— regrettably unsystematic—of an ill-kept garden; the noble houses of England were so well trimmed that by 1485 only twenty-nine lay lords answered Henry VII's first parliamentary writ.[22]

There is no clearer lesson in kingship than this allegory in Shakespeare, and no other didactic intrusion like it. The ideal relationship between sovereign and subject, then, presupposes the sovereign's possession and liberal use of the gardner's scythe. It is not a pleasant lesson. But it is an accurate one. And the poet, in three more plays, will explore his lesson both fully and for all time.

Scene is most important, writes that "a good ruler, it is intimated, is like a good gardener, participating in the fructifying activities of his king-dom instead of merely standing off and watching them. . . . (p. 160)— a judgment that I neither concur in nor wholly understand. If one equates king and gardener, one must deal with execution, not exalted participation.

Similarly Tillyard: "In passing, for it is not my immediate concern, let me add that the gardener gives both the pattern and the moral of the play (p. 250)." While Tillyard is quite right as far as he goes, the allegory does quite as well for all the history plays as it does for *Richard II*.

[22]Trevelyan, vol. I, p. 26.

V ॐ The Gardener's King
1 and 2 *Henry IV*

I
N his treatment of Henry Bolingbroke, later Henry IV, Shakespeare created the wholly public figure. Even Henry's griefs are political; he mourns the absence of the prince far more than he mourns the absence of the son. And precisely because Henry IV is Shakespeare's most complete political portrait, we undervalue him when we regard him as only a symptom of that disease which afflicts the body politic.[1]

Like Julius Caesar, Henry IV dominates events which survive him, and near the end of his life he very nearly attains the tragic dimension of self-realization—except that his self-realization, like his life, is more political than personal. His long and sullen shadow is all-pervading: at the tavern Falstaff talks compulsively of his gallows,[2] and Henry has already festooned the gates of London with the heads of his antagonists.

[1]The student of these plays ought to notice the opposing, because more doctrinal, view of Henry IV eloquently summarized by H. M. Richmond: "Shakespeare systematically identifies in Bolingbroke that new type of amoral perversity to whom success and title will necessarily go in the modern political life that has been cut off from medieval cosmic values. He devotes the rest of his political plays to the investigation of whether such a personality, and the environment it creates, are in any way compatible with the practice of the archaic virtues and the Christian ideal." (*Shakespeare,* p. 140.)

[2]A compulsion first noticed by Dover Wilson in *The Fortunes of Falstaff,* p. 40.

And our reaction to Henry is curiously dualized. In *Richard II*
he is the embodiment of the gardener's allegorical depiction of
the ideal king; in *1 Henry IV*, alternating between pious, politic
prevarication and the exercise of his iron will, he is hugely preferable to the chaotic alternative conjunction against which he
strives. It is only in *2 Henry IV* that the full horror of Henry
Bolingbroke is developed: his deathbed gift is the treachery of
Gaultree forest, and his dying is marred by the imperfect but
only possible reconciliation between this king, weary of life but
politically insatiable, and his son, the prince who is as eager for
the dawning of a new day as is that prince's audience.

The key to Henry IV, and through him to the plays which
bear his name, lies in understanding his changing dimensions.
It is ignored by no one that Shakespeare devoted three plays
to the education and reign of Henry V; that the poet devoted
precisely the same number of plays to the polity of Henry IV
is too seldom noticed, and that he devoted a fourth play, *Henry
V,* in part at least to the aftereffects of Henry IV's polity is
noticed rarely or not at all. But the spirit of Henry IV is as
much present at Agincourt as is the spirit of Julius Caesar at
Philippi.

We have noted that each of Shakespeare's English kings is
not only an antidote to the ills of the previous reign, but also—
witness Richard III, Edward IV, and Henry VI—an unsuccessful antidote. None of the kings tested—except Prince Henry in
King John and Henry VII, for reasons both political and dramatic—meets the problems of his successor satisfactorily. In
this sense we may regard the wounds of England as running
sores; none of the cures, from John to Henry Bolingbroke, heals
the wounds.

When, then, we are unable to find in personal terms a dramatic solution to dramatic problems, we begin to look for
dogma; in *Richard II* we find it. The Gardener, who represents, as we have noted, the sole direct didactic intrusion in
these plays, gives us dogma: rule by the ax, by the sword, by
the whip. Tested against this dogma—perhaps advanced in
despair and quickly abandoned, or perhaps ironically advanced

as a flawed but conceivable theory which must collapse of its own ugly weight—Henry IV is, in *Richard II*, the ideal king until he, like the Richards and like John, is ensnared by the consequences of his own acts.

But to establish such a polity as the Gardener suggests requires a man of considerable—and consistent—cruel force. "Thus it is well," wrote Machiavelli, "to seem merciful, faithful, humane, sincere, religious, and also to be so; but you must have the mind so disposed that when it is needful to be otherwise you may be able to change to the opposite qualities."[3] The significant difference between Henry IV and Richard II is that while each uses the same weapons—banishment, confiscation, execution—the policies of Richard are determined by whimsical caprices as monumental as his vanity, whereas Henry IV with cold calculation alternates piety and murder, mercy and the mailed fist, so frequently that his policy appears as mixed as his metaphors. To his suggestible executioner, Sir Pierce of Exton, pious Henry cries: "With Cain go wander through the shades of night/ And never show thy head by day nor light" (*Richard II*, V, vi), but the deadly admission that "They love not poison that do poison need" is already there, to stain the reign of the king and color the judgment of his peers.

Mercy for Carlisle. Mercy for Aumerle; "I pardon him," Henry declaims to the distraught Duke and Duchess of York, "as God shall pardon me." (*Richard II*, V, iii.) But death to Richard—and, at the hands of Northumberland and Fitzwater, death to Oxford, Salisbury, Blunt, Kent, Brocas, and Sir Bennet Seely. To his executioners Henry says his thanks in two of the crudest couplets Shakespeare ever penned. To Northumberland: "We thank thee, gentle Percy, for thy pains;/ And to thy worth will add right worthy gains." And to Fitzwater: "Thy pains, Fitzwater, shall not be forgot;/ Right noble is thy merit, well I wot." (*Richard II*, V, vi.)

The king is indeed crude and pious, remorseless and merciful, a master of that art of calculated turnabout so pitilessly described by Machiavelli. It is not of course by the fact of

[3]*The Prince*, p. 102.

murders, even judicial murders, that Henry is disturbed; he, the woeful metaphoric growth that takes for nourishment his subjects' blood, is moved from exaltation to pious remorse only by the blood of his predecessor—his "buried fear." (*Richard II,* V, vi.)[4]

And well may Shakespeare's Henry be moved to piety, however false, for here the Lancastrian king is tripped by that same fact of royal survival—that the king is not king while rivals live— over which Plantagenet John and Yorkist Richard stumbled. Richard dreams, and apparitions appear to him; John, like Richard II a hyperbolic representation of emotion run rampant, lashes out at what he supposes to be his deed's living representation. To Hubert—innocent, ugly Hubert—John cries:

> Hadst not thou been by,
> A fellow by the hand of nature mark'd,
> Quoted, and sign'd to do a deed of shame,
> This murder had not come into my mind . . .
> (*King John,* IV, ii.)

As Henry to Exton, so John to Hubert: "Out of my sight, and never see me more!" (*King John,* IV, ii.) And Henry mumbles darkly about a pilgrimage. But to no purpose, for if it is to Henry IV's credit that he, unlike John and Richard II, had sense enough not to seek—in his lifetime—the solution to domestic troubles in foreign war, it is history's, and Shakespeare's, verdict upon Henry IV that from the entrance of Exton with Richard's coffin to the report of victory at Gaultree forest, Henry is never out of domestic trouble. Unlike the sad, really pious Henry VI who was, by fits and starts, to succeed him after his son's brief blaze, Henry IV is able to keep his throne, but the margin of retention is as narrow as the path to Shrewsbury is straight and clearly marked.

[4]A "buried fear" of which I think Goddard makes too much; he tends to lose the political Henry within the dimensions of the psychological Henry: "The spirit of the man who once banished him and whom he had deposed enters his body and deposes and banishes his own spirit." (*The Meaning of Shakespeare,* p. 165.)

And Richard, rendered impotent by events and prophetic by the vision of his doom, has pointed the way to Shrewsbury even in the moment of his cousin's glory:

> Northumberland, thou ladder wherewithal
> The mounting Bolingbroke ascends my throne,
> The time shall not be many hours of age
> More than it is, ere foul sin gathering head
> Shall break into corruption. Thou shalt think,
> Though he divide the realm and give thee half,
> It is too little, helping him to all;
> And he shall think that thou, which know'st the way
> To plant unrightful kings, wilt know again,
> Being ne'er so little urg'd, another way
> To pluck him headlong from the usurped throne.
>
> (*Richard II*, V, i.)

This is a process all too familiar to us—more a link with the plays which have gone before than to the plays which will come. Remember Warwick and Edward IV, Richard of Gloucester and Edward IV, Buckingham and Richard III. Richard II, inspired by rage, adduces an historical axiom: "The love of wicked men converts to fear/ That fear to hate, and hate turns one or both/ To worthy danger and deserved death." (*Richard II*, V, i.) Richard is unaware that he, torn by Northumberland not so much from the arms of his queen as from his recitation of the sad circumstances of his projected dying, has characterized his own relationship with his uncle Woodstock and his faithful Mowbray. But his prophecy and his murder chart the course of the reign of Henry IV: from treason to treason, from battlefield to battlefield. Holinshed's conclusion is Richard's prophecy fulfilled:

And to speake a truth, no marvell it was, if manie envied the prosperous state of King Henrie, with it was evident inough to the world, that he had with wrong usurped the crowne, but also cruellie procured his death; for the which undoubtedlie, both he and his posteritie tasted such troubles, as put them still in danger of their states, till their direct succeeding line was quite rooted out of the contrarie faction, as in Henrie the sixth and Edward the fourth it may appeare.[5]

The only solution, it would appear, for the problems of Henry IV's reign as they evolve is that sort of total insensitivity to the consequences of evil but necessary actions to which Richard III pretends in the early acts of his play. And in Henry's ironic restraint with the babbling family of York we suspect great strength—the greater in that, unlike the early strength of Richard III, it may be in fact concealed. In the scene before Flint Castle we find in Henry an unsuspected, lewd humor which breaks his hypocritical obsequiousness with great ironic force:

> Be he [Richard] the fire, I'll be the yielding water;
> The rage be his, whilst on the earth I rain
> My waters—on the earth, and not on him.
>   (*Richard II*, III, iii.)

The spectacle of grim—and, up to this point, humorless—Bolingbroke determining to urinate upon the earth rather than upon the Lord's Anointed strikes us as praiseworthy contrast to Richard's grandiose pretension.

Here, then, is the Gardener's king, and Machiavelli's: utterly without illusion, his remorse nothing but rhetorical posture, cold, cynical, willing not only to have done what must be done but also to mask his instrument behind exile and to obscure his judicial murders in the haze of a false crusade. A harsh remedy, in sum, but a perfect one. Save of course for the fact that all men, in life and in drama, may be balked of their purposes by the consequences of their acts. But not Bolingbroke—yet.

That part of the reign of Henry IV presented in *1 Henry IV* is an exercise in crude strength fallen to tactics. If a king is to be measured by the stability of his kingdom, Henry IV is no model, for his kingdom is, as Richard prophesied, a hatchnest of rebellions; but if a king is to be judged simply by his durability, Henry is quite remarkably successful—especially when compared with his Shakespearean predecessors. And if a king

[5]*Chronicles*, p. 188.

may also be measured by the subtlety with which he, matured in crisis and brought to greatness by remarkable coincidence of desire and opportunity, forces and then deals with the issues of his day, Henry is superb.

"So shaken as we are, so wan with care" (*1 Henry IV*, I, i), begins the monarch who, under the guise of a concern for civil war to be offset by a specious crusade, is about to provoke civil war again. Worcester is sent for in private, "For more is to be said and to be done/ Than out of anger can be uttered." (*1 Henry IV*, I, i.) The business at hand is rebellion, and the king, astute, still without illusion, is no less acute in his recognition that the revolt of his kingmakers is inevitable, than was prophetic Richard. He is every inch the king:

> My blood hath been too cold and temperate,
> Unapt to stir at these indignities,
> And you found me; for accordingly
> You tread upon my patience.
> (*1 Henry IV*, I, iii.)

And Henry is as good as his word. Worcester, to whom both treason and presumption are as native as breath, is dismissed from his presence with little grace but much majesty: "Worcester, get thee gone; for I do see/ Danger and disobedience in thine eye." The Percys fare no better: "My Lord Northumberland,/ We license your departure with your son./ Send us your prisoners, or you'll hear of it." (*1 Henry IV*, I, iii.)

The battle of Shrewsbury is on, and the process of its making is as neat a tactical exercise as there is in all Shakespeare. The Percys have looked for cause to rebel, and the king has given them cause; but the king is at the zenith of his power, and the rebels are forced, when the insensate, mindless fury of fanatic Hotspur is abated, to pursue unlikely targets in distasteful ways. Worcester will ". . . steal to Glendower and Lord Mortimer"; Worcester tells Northumberland, ". . . into the bosom creep/ Of that same noble prelate, well belov'd/ The Archbishop." It remains for Hotspur, the ageless, arrested adolescent, happily to cap our reaction to the conspiracy: "I smell it. Upon my life, it will do well." (*1 Henry IV*, I, iii.)

And smell it does. The Percys, seeking allies, divide as much
as they add; the victory of their faction would involve frag-
mentation of the kingdom:

> GLEND. Come, here's the map. Shall we divide our right
>   According to our threefold order ta'en?
> MORT.   The Archdeacon hath divided it
>   Into three limits very equally.
>   (*1 Henry IV,* III, i.)

In this division lies the weakness of the plot against Henry, for,
of the three parties, only the Percys have to fight. Glendower,
according to the agreement, receives Wales, which he already
possesses. Mortimer has a refuge with Glendower. Northumberland deserts his son, and Glendower, who would have fought
for Richard, will not fight for Percy. Hotspur has lost the
battle before it is fairly begun.

Before Shrewsbury, the king's offer of clemency to the rebels
is perverted into defiance by Worcester, but Worcester's reason-
ing has the ring of truth:

> It is not possible, it cannot be,
> The King should keep his word in loving us.
> He will suspect us still, and find a time
> To punish this offence in other faults.
>   (*1 Henry IV,* V, ii.)

Certainly Henry expects his offer of clemency to be rejected,
for upon his son's remark that "The Douglas and the Hotspur
both together/ Are confident against the world in arms," the
king orders: "Hence, therefore, every leader to his charge,/ For,
on their answer, will we set on them . . ." (*1 Henry IV,* V, i.)
But one suspects that Henry, who has done as much to provoke Shrewsbury as have the rebels, would attack whatever the
answer, for absolute, final victory at Shrewsbury is vital to him.
The king and Worcester have taken each other's measure
shrewdly, and one must destroy the other. And if treachery is
the essence of the earl, so duplicity has become the essence of
the king. "What art thou," cries Douglas in desperation, as
at last he encounters the king himself, "That counterfeit'st the

person of a king?" (*1 Henry IV*, V, iv.) And earlier Hotspur
has told Douglas, "The King hath many marching in his coats."
(*1 Henry IV*, V, iii.) The king is no coward, as his fight with
Douglas evidences; but he is—and this is his tragedy—mired in
the methods of his predecessors.

To the list of the executed we add—and we do not regret
it—Worcester and Vernon. But we pause at the dimensions of
the list. The king wished always to rule, and his conception
of the kingship was in its way no less exalted, if far more practical, than his shallow cousin's; we may presume he wished to
rule well. He has provoked a rebellion which, had he procrasti-
nated, might have destroyed him; while he left to his opponents
the choice of weapons, his peremptory dismissals retained for
him the choice of time and place. He chooses to attack, and
to attack immediately; we take his offers of clemency no more
seriously than does Worcester.[6] In this specious clemency and
abrupt attack there is the touch of genius—as at Shrewsbury,
in the device of the many coats, there is the touch of the
monarch whose instinct for self-preservation is no less regal for
being thorough, since that instinct is not mixed with cowardice.

Yet Henry, no matter how many his gifts and how right his
instincts, is able only to subdue, not to rule. His weakness is
the very human one of misunderstanding his brilliant, deceptive,
multipurposed son; no scene in *1 Henry IV* better underscores
the totality of the king as a political creature, and the degree to
which the weight of care rather than the weight of his crown
has blunted his customarily ready wit, than his reply to Hal's
protestations of loyalty: "A hundred thousand rebels die in this."
(III, ii.) Even the return of the prodigal is a political event,
and the reconciliation of father and son is a military alliance.

[6]I cannot agree with Traversi's rendering of this scene. "Both sides,"
he writes, "at heart desire peace—the rebels because they know they are
not strong enough to win, the king because unity is the substance of the
royal vocation and because experience has taught him that the divisions
in his kingdom are not such as battle, even victorious, can resolve."
(*Shakespeare*, p. 96.) It seems to me that the text amply justifies the
assumption that Henry knows that the spirit of rebellion is quelled only
by the death of the rebellious. And surely Hotspur's bellicosity, like
Worcester's deceit, is boundless.

It is a sad moment, both for the devious father who misunder-
stands, and also for the son who understands all too well.

By this much, then, are Henry's dimensions shrunken in
the first of the two plays which bear his name. As the poet's
interest in abstraction has lessened, so has the breadth, if not
the depth, of the portrayal of the king; the anti-hero, Falstaff,
has entered, and the king, the abstracted iron man, does not
appear well by contrast. A new generation, that of the princes
and Hotspur, has entered, and the king is suddenly old. Henry
has known the value of contrast—"Thus did I keep my person
fresh and new" (*1 Henry IV*, III, ii), he bitterly tells his son,
before making his unflattering estimation of chivalry's truant,
an estimate more fatherly than correct. But an old king is not
an old Falstaff, for the king is plagued by the vices of his age,
rather than, like Falstaff, relishing the vices of youth into an
ageless antiquity.

It is the tragedy of the wholly political man that he must,
in time, be superseded. And *1 Henry IV* makes the king, with
all his gifts, look old and his supercession not only inevitable
but desirable. It remains for Henry, the greatest of Shakespeare's English kings, only to compose a weary epitaph.

Proper understanding of the second part of *Henry IV* is
dependent upon the recognition that in it the Lord Chief Justice represents, far more than does the king, the arm of royal
authority.[7] It is the Lord Chief Justice to whom Henry V turns,
briefly, for both the mantle of legitimate authority and the
harsh rhetoric of the rejection of his former friend; and it is the
Lord Chief Justice who serves as the check upon Falstaff's
depredations, as well as being Falstaff's foil.[8]

The king is now a stationary figure. Old, ill, increasingly
dependent upon his sons, he broods:

[7]A recognition for which we are indebted to Dover Wilson, who, partly
because the focus of his discussion is so unwaveringly kept upon Falstaff,
does not treat the importance of the Lord Chief Justice to the political
structure of the play. (*Fortunes of Falstaff*, pp. 98–99.)

[8]Dover Wilson: "And if the language of the speech [rejection of Fal-
staff] sounds formal and homiletic, that is because Hal is learning to
speak, not as Bradley complains, 'like a clergyman,' but like the Chief
Justice . . ." (*Fortunes of Falstaff*, p. 121.)

> It is but eight years since
> This Percy was the man nearest my soul,
> Who like a brother toil'd in my affairs
> And laid his love and life under my foot;
> Yea, for my sake, even to the eyes of Richard
> Gave him defiance.   (2 *Henry IV*, III, i.)

There the reminiscences of an old man, coupled with his meditations: "Uneasy lies the head that wears a crown." The king's reflections on the state of his kingdom are grim:

> Then you perceive the body of our kingdom
> How foul it is; what rank diseases grow,
> And with what danger, near the heart of it.
>   (2 *Henry IV*, III, i.)

Warwick, oddly comforting, regards Northumberland's treachery (Henry has quoted Richard's prophecy of it) as ". . . a history in all men's lives/ Figuring the nature of the times deceas'd . . . a necessary form." Henry's reply is an anguished question: "Are these things then necessities?" (III, i.)

And his resolve to meet the necessities is no less firm than it was in the time of Richard—a time which, even here, the deceit so native in him compels him to describe as that occasion when ". . . necessity so bow'd the state,/ That I and greatness were compell'd to kiss." (2 *Henry IV*, III, i.) Indeed "necessity" is central not just to the scene but to the reign; for the Gardener's conception of duty, and the iron will which must accompany that conception, are with the king yet. Henry may not, as the Archbishop of York observes at Gaultree, ". . . so precisely weed this land/ As his misdoubts present occasion." (2 *Henry IV*, IV ,i.) The archbishop, in his pastoral imagery, recalls the garden and its Gardener—and also the image of the king fructified by the blood of his subjects. It is not a comfortable duality, but we may not ignore it. And of Henry we must recognize that it is his health, not his will, which fails: "Only, we want a little personal strength." (2 *Henry IV*, IV, iv.)

But the strength is not forthcoming, and the ironies of this king's dying are massive. To Jerusalem indeed he goes, to the Jerusalem Chamber, where he warns the royal princes about

their elder brother's counselors. Despite Warwick's misinterpre-
tation, the king, now fitfully clearsighted, warns not of the
company of the tavern but of the diseases, "rage and hot blood,"
of the Prince of Wales' disordered soul—not of his low com-
panions but of his intemperate nature:

> Yet notwithstanding, being incens'd, he's flint,
> As humorous as winter, and as sudden
> As flaws congealed in the spring of day.
> His temper, therefore, must be well observ'd.
>   (2 *Henry IV*, IV, iv.)

His warning delivered and news of the victory at Gaultree
forest received, the king asks that he be removed from what will
prove to have been his nearest approach to the Holy Land, although at the end, his breath spent, he will ask to be returned
to it again. It remains only that he die, estranged again from
his son and then at last reconciled to him—in a reconciliation
not really between world-weary father and son, but between
a dying king and an eager heir.

"Thou seek'st," Henry warns his son, "the greatness that
will overwhelm thee." (2 *Henry IV*, IV, v.) The king lashes
the prince with the record of the young man's venal sins, and
then, in a series of revelations even here more political than
personal, reveals to him the foundations of his own polity. His
lines are heavy with guilt, but a guilt oddly free of self-recrimi-
nation; Henry does not regret what he has done—only that it
did not turn out better:

> God knows, my son,
> By what by-paths and indirect crook'd ways
> I met this crown; and I myself know well
> How troublesome it sat upon my head.
>   (2 *Henry IV*, IV, v.)

This is not remorse; it is, like his soliloquy on sleep, a series of
factual recognitions. By this degree—his intense, narrow practi-
cality—Henry falls short of the tragic dimension; by this same
degree, however, Henry as king has avoided the relentless alienating remorse which at last rendered Richard III the magnifi-

cent Knight, careless of consequences. Henry is never a Knight, nor magnificent; he is always the Gardener's king—with a list of judicial murders far longer than Richard III's, albeit neither personally performed nor so close in blood. And Henry, the eternal public man even in death,

> . . . had a purpose now
> To lead out many to the Holy Land
> Lest rest and lying still might make them look
> Too near unto my state.   (2 *Henry IV*, IV, v.)

At last piety and hope are coupled: "How I came by the crown, O God forgive;/ And grant it may with thee in true peace live!" We distrust the piety, but—despite his own warnings—we join the Gardener's king in this last wish.

VI ❧ The Shakespearean Bestiary
1 and 2 *Henry IV* and *Henry V*

I T is against the shrewd wit and immense anti-heroism of Sir John Falstaff that the serious actions of the serious characters in the first and second parts of *Henry IV* are tested. Beside him, his venality so grossly exposed that his immensity itself becomes venality condoned, kings and princes and judges are reduced to the petty. King Henry is, as we have noted, denied the tragic dimension by his intense narrowness; Hotspur's uncle Worcester, with the king, may be permitted to define the political world of *1* and *2 Henry IV*.

It may be that Shakespeare had tired of princes and kings, or that, having postulated through the Gardener a notion of perfection too grim to be palatable and too dependent upon mechanistic efficiency to be dramatic, he had tired of theories. Beside Falstaff, the world of the court is flat and dull; we tire of the theft of the throne, but look forward to the robbery at Gadshill. Falstaff is an altered perspective, a new prism through which to see the world of affairs; his venality, at once so gross and so much less in scope than that of the political characters, is endearing by contrast: ". . . when he runs away or lies down he is more adorable than any hero 'facing fearful odds.' . . . a hero run hugely to seed; he is actually heavier and bigger than the heaviest and biggest true colossus or hero. He is in that respect, physically, a mock-hero. . . . And because of this mean-

ingless, unmasculine immensity he always occupies the centre
of the stage, he is the great landmark in any scene where he
is. It all means nothing, and is a physical sham and trick put
on the eye. And so he becomes the embodiment of bluff and
worldly practice, the colossus of the little."[1]

Falstaff is both pygmy and giant, an ultimate burlesque.
If in Hal, later Henry V, the union of lion and fox is achieved,
that union is by Falstaff pantomimed into the ludicrous; Shrewsbury is rendered a comedy rather than a setting for heroics, and
the dominion by guile of the strong over the weak is reduced
to absurdity in Gloucestershire by the tyranny of the fat knight
over puny Justice Shallow.

"A prince being thus obliged to know well how to act as
a beast," wrote Machiavelli, "must imitate the fox and the
lion, for the lion cannot protect himself from traps, and the
fox cannot defend himself from wolves. One must therefore be
a fox to recognize traps and a lion to frighten wolves."[2] Falstaff is the anti-lion at Shrewsbury, the anti-fox as he waits for
the procession of Henry V to pass. He recognizes no traps, he
frightens no wolves. But there are lions and wolves all about
him. Hotspur is the lion, hugely decayed; the vulpine king sets
traps. And Falstaff, his innocence untouched by his venality
because his faith also is as immense as his bulk, dies heartbroken,
betrayed by motives and forces which he is too grand to understand. Falstaff in his eternal youth could not know, as Machiavelli did in his eternal age, that "the first impression that one
gets of a ruler and his brains is from seeing the men that he
has about him."[3] By this rule, Falstaff must go, and go he
does—to the Fleet, at the order of the lord chief justice. And
it is no accident that the chief justice is accompanied by Prince
John of Lancaster, a pairing of rectitude and expediency which
go oddly well together.

[1]Lewis, *The Lion and the Fox*, p. 227.

[2]*The Prince*, p. 101. The student of these plays is referred to Ribner's
comment: "To dismiss, as Tillyard does, Machiavelli and all he brought
to historical method as lying 'outside the main sixteenth-century interest'
is clearly shortsighted." (*The English History Play*, p. 12.)

[3]*The Prince*, p. 124.

It is in Falstaff's erstwhile companion, the prince, that the lion and the fox are joined, and Falstaff's dramatic function is to burlesque that union. The lion in Prince Hal will lead us from the field of Shrewsbury to Agincourt, and the fox points the way from his first soliloquy to the cumbersome, acquisitive wooing of Katharine. Shakespeare devoted three plays to the boy Hal and to the king he becomes, but the scope of the plays owes far more to the intoduction of Falstaff than to the figure of the prince.[4]

Falstaff is a kind of life, an embodiment of anarchic vitality; he snores, but kings cannot sleep; he laughs—and as his bulk trembles with the pleasure of life lived fully, we are rudely forced by his creator back into the dimensions of the purely practical. If we reduce Falstaff to the political, we have simply a self-seeking anarchist; if, however, we surrender—as Hal never does—to his vision and to our vision of him, we are, as Falstaff is, free. Falstaff is a holiday; a vacation from affairs, from business, from the practical. "He is a point of contact between two worlds. In him, the larger life of humanity, at its most genial and exuberant, is brought into touch with the narrow life of the public person at its most calculating and unscrupulous."[5]

And all that is without scruple, all that is dictated by calculation pure, is subsumed within that prince who hides himself behind Falstaff's bulk. The most remarkable facet of Henry, Prince of Wales, is his utter fidelity to the spirit and letter of his first soliloquy.[6] Prince Henry's exposition of his objective and method is a harsh contrast to the pleasantries of the tavern

[4]And the theatricality of *Henry* V is dependent upon Falstaff's disappearance; not, as Dover Wilson suggested, because Will Kempe left the company (*Fortunes of Falstaff*, p. 125), but because: "one touch of Falstaff, in daylight, would have effectively destroyed all touch of Harry in the night." (Palmer, p. 227.)

[5]Palmer, p. 184.

[6]"Everything, from the first soliloquy on, proves that the prince not only craved renown but craved it in its most theatrical form." (Goddard, p. 190. Nothing since Wilson's *The Fortunes of Falstaff* has, in my judgment, so enriched the dialogue surrounding these three plays as have the essays of this astute, if enthusiastic, Freudian.)

which precede it; the soliloquy, however, is no less thorough a
revelation of the spirit of the man than is the initial soliloquy
of Richard III. Prince Henry does not have Richard's dimensions, for he is not his own comic foil; the prince, unlike the
duke, cannot observe himself. But his observations of his time,
his place in those times, and how his place is to be achieved
are both keen and frank:

> I know you all, and will a while uphold
> The unyok'd humour of your idleness.
> Yet herein will I imitate the sun,
> Who doth permit the base contagious clouds
> To smother up his beauty from the world,
> That when he please again to be himself
> Being wanted, he may be more wond'red at
> By breaking through the foul and ugly mists
> Of vapours that did seem to strangle him.
> If all the year were playing holidays,
> To sport would be as tedious as to work;
> But when they seldom come, they wish'd for come,
> And nothing pleaseth but rare accidents.
> So, when this loose behaviour I throw off
> And pay the debt I never promised,
> By how much better than my word I am,
> By so much shall I falsify men's hopes;
> And like bright metal on a sullen ground,
> My reformation, glitt'ring o'er my fault,
> Shall show more goodly and attract more eyes
> Than that which hath no foil to set it off.
> I'll so offend, to make offense a skill,
> Redeeming time when men think least I will.
>
> (1 Henry IV, I, ii.)

Like Richard II, Prince Henry compares himself to the sun;
like Richard III, who in the famous strawberry scene masks
his purposes behind his deformity, Prince Henry has adopted
disguises. Falstaff and his companion of the tavern are the "base
contagious clouds," the "foul and ugly mists" through which
Henry, the allegorical "sun," will eventually break. And, like
his father, Prince Henry—hardly at this point the familiar "Hal"
of the tavern—will depend upon contrast. His reformation will,

we are told, so overshadow his faults that he will, in the times
to come, seem better than he is. And, by the time of *Henry V,*
the "bright metal" to which the prince has referred shows very
brightly indeed:

> Never was such a sudden scholar made;
> Never came reformation in a flood
> With such a heady currance, scouring faults;
> Nor never hydra-headed wilfulness
> So soon did lose his seat, and all at once,
> As in this king.   (*Henry V,* I, i.)

This then is Prince Henry's method: the sudden transfor-
mation, a kind of secular alchemy in which the base is made
precious, and made to seem more precious yet by the celerity
of the transmutation. A clever process—yet not beyond the
capacity of the bright student of his father's methods, as easily
seen as heard confessed:

> Thus did I keep my person fresh and new,
> My presence, like a robe pontifical . . .
> The skipping king, he ambled up and down
> With shallow jesters and rash bavin wits,
> Soon kindled and soon burnt . . .
> (*1 Henry IV,* III, ii.)

So the prince, a legitimate heir rather than a usurper, unlike
his royal predecessor Richard III in being of sound body but
most like the malformed usurper in the fundamental unsound-
ness of his nature, will play the dissembler. And he does it
so well that he fools even his father. Prince Henry is the perfection of the fox.

But with his father's state and his own succession imperiled,
the truant to chivalry must, like the prodigal, return.[7] It is,
ironically, the "coward upon instinct" who informs the prince
that the rebels are up; whereupon the disguise of the tavern
is shed with considerable dispatch. Falstaff warns the prince

[7]The reader should note Dover Wilson's shrewd rendering of the
theme of "Riot and the Prodigal Prince" in *The Fortunes of Falstaff,*
pp. 17–25.

about the passing of youth: ". . . for though the camomile, the more it is trodden on the faster it grows, yet youth, the more it is wasted the sooner it wears." And the player-king, "in 'King Cambyses'" vein, defends himself: ". . . there is virtue in that Falstaff; him keep with, the rest banish!" (*1 Henry IV*, II, iv.)

But the prince is eager to play the king—and not in Cambyses' vein. Attacked, the "villainous abominable misleader of youth, Falstaff, that old white-bearded Satan" defends himself by sharply distinguishing his own venality from real wickedness:

But to say I know more harm to him than in myself, were to say more than I know. That he is old, the more the pity, his white hairs do witness it; but that he is, saving your reverence, a whoremaster, that I utterly deny. If sack and sugar be a fault, God help the wicked! If to be old and merry be a sin, then many an old host that I know is damn'd. If to be fat be to be hated, then Pharaoh's lean kine are to be loved. No, my good lord; banish Peto, banish Bardolph, banish Poins; but for sweet Jack Falstaff, kind Jack Falstaff, true Jack Falstaff, valiant Jack Falstaff, and therefore more valiant, being, as he is, old Jack Falstaff, banish not him thy Harry's company. Banish plump Jack, and banish all the world.

(*1 Henry IV*, II, iv.)

And in the prince's cold, determined reply, "I do, I will," occurs the rejection of Falstaff.[8] But Falstaff is not quite finished: "never call a true piece of gold a counterfeit. Thou art essentially mad without seeming so." There is much of counterfeiting in this play, and madness later on; but Falstaff here is rejected—and he feels it. In his next appearance Sir John is much diminished: "Well, I'll repent and that suddenly, while I am in some liking. I shall be out of heart shortly, and then I shall have no strength to repent." (*1 Henry IV*, III, iii.)

[8]Of this scene, the most crucial in *1 Henry IV*, Goddard wrote that ". . . what Shakespeare is giving us here is a rehearsal of the rejection of Falstaff." (*The Meaning of Shakespeare*, p. 207.) But the scene is more than a "rehearsal" of the rejection; it is the rejection, for neither Falstaff nor Prince Henry is the same after it. Dover Wilson ignores the importance of this scene entirely: "we must hence, and leave it unpicked, alas because—blessed scene—it raises no problms that need disentangling." (*The Fortunes of Falstaff*, p. 56.)

But to repent is not in Falstaff's nature, and he is no longer "in some liking." The formal rejection will come later: public, brutal, couched in the harsh, homiletic rhetoric borrowed for the occasion from the lord chief justice, and flawed, even in the moment of the banishment not only of Falstaff but of "fool-born jest," with precisely that—an ill-timed, fool-born jest:

> I know thee not, old man; fall to thy prayers.
> How ill white hairs become a fool and jester!
> I have long dreamt of such a kind of man,
> So surfeit-swell'd, so old, and so profane;
> But, being awak'd, I do despise my dream.
> Make less thy body hence, and more thy grace;
> Leave gormandizing; know the grave doth gape
> For thee thrice wider than for other men.
> Reply not to me with a fool-born jest.
>   (2 Henry IV, V, v.)

It falls to shattered Sir John to complete the images of disguise; broken, he reflects first that he owes Shallow a thousand pounds, and then protests, "Look you, he must seem thus to the world. . . . This that you heard was but a colour . . . I shall be sent for soon at night." (2 Henry IV, V, v.) The next most devastating commentary upon this, only the second of Henry V's appearances as king, is that treacherous John of Lancaster approves it so heartily: "I like this fair proceeding of the king's." (2 Henry IV, V, v.)

That, then, is the public Henry V: harsh, rectitudinous, a grandstand performer.[9] He has, as he promised, redeemed time—and when men least thought he would. He has banished Falstaff, who has warned the prince of the fragility of youth; he has reassured his brothers, whom the dying king has warned against his temperament. It is an auspicious public beginning— as Richard III's might have been, did we not know that the

___

[9] In his discussion in 1943 of the rejection of Falstaff, Dover Wilson reveals his immense topicality in a scarcely veiled condemnation of the Duke of Windsor. (P. 123.) His topicality is less pleasantly evidenced in his remarks regarding the reception of John Masefield's attack upon the character of Prince Henry as "reinforced by the reigning pacificism of the early twentieth century." (P. 7.)

Duke of Gloucester posed between bishops merely political, and read the Devil's book.

Prince Henry is no less an adroit performer in private than in public. Of all men living, it is Henry IV whom the prince must dupe, and he does it superbly, in language native to the king himself:

> I will redeem all this on Percy's head,
> And in the closing of some glorious day,
> Be bold to tell you that I am your son;
> When I will wear a garment all of blood
> And stain my favors in a bloody mask . . .
>
> (*1 Henry IV*, III, iii.)

Such a process of recognition is perhaps understandable to a king who has metaphorically presented himself as a plant nourished in his subjects' blood, but the rhetoric is as cold as the prince. "Percy is but my factor, good my lord . . ." continues Prince Henry, introducing the shoddiest, Falstaff excepted, of all his bargains with Commodity.

The stammering Hotspur is an anachronism, but he does not displease; his challenge to Henry is addressed, with a clarity rare in the intemperate, to the spirit of the fledgling lion: "I can no longer brook thy vanities." And with Falstaff cheering (thereby bringing to this combat the faintly ludicrous note which he brings to all Prince Henry's heroics), Hotspur is slain. Hotspur is "food—for worms, brave Percy," and, ironically but with considerable truth, the prince observes, "This earth which bears thee dead/ Bears not alive so stout a gentleman." Scant courtesy is paid to the elephantine corpse which lies nearby:

> O, I should have a heavy miss of thee
> If I were much in love with vanity!
> Death hath not struck so fat a deer to-day,
> Though many dearer, in this bloody fray.
>
> (*1 Henry IV*, V, iv.)

We ought not to make too much of an obvious theatrical contrivance, but the Prince's subjunctives are as suggestive as his pun is lame.[10] And the Prince who has cropped Hotspur's garlands has not forsworn vanities; he has simply altered roles.

Falstaff, rising, returns to the theme of the counterfeit, having already noticed the distasteful aspect honor bears on the late Sir Walter Blunt. And while Shrewsbury's satirist is not behindhand in claiming more than his share of the victory, he has rendered the battle itself less than serious. Our delight at Shrewsbury does not consist in relish of the king's victory, though we approve it, or of Hal's heroics; Shrewsbury is Shakespeare's happiest field because Falstaff, having expended duty with his men, is there to debunk the battle. Dynastic wars, the attitude of Falstaff suggests, are of great seriousness only to those dynastically involved. Falstaff came to play, and exits carrying huge burdens—the body of Hotspur, and a happily brief notion of repentance.

Dover Wilson wrote that ". . . viewing *Henry IV* as a whole, we may label part I the Return to Chivalry; part II as the Atonement with Justice."[11] Yet we may note that it is Falstaff's function in the first part of *Henry IV* rather to burlesque chivalry than to return us to it: Prince Henry kills chivalry's mirror, Hotspur, after reducing his dimensions to those of the "factor"; Henry IV, as frequently sinning as sinned against, has provoked Shrewsbury as much in the recognition that the king must rid himself—and quickly—of the agents by which he came to power as through his fear of the Earl of March; the rebels, who would rid England of its king and then fragment England, are to politics what Hotspur's stutter is to rhetoric. And Falstaff—on the aspect of honor, or counterfieting, or having "misused the king's press damnably" (*1 Henry IV*, V, ii)—makes us laugh at it all. The function of the anti-hero is, after all, to satirize false heroics.

[10]Dover Wilson quotes Prince Henry's pun, having admitted that "what there is of affection is mainly retrospective. . . . after Shrewsbury Falstaff is never again on the same terms with his patron." (*Fortunes of Falstaff*, p. 67.) It seems to me that Henry's pun is as savage as ill-wrought; we have already contended that the breach between Falstaff and his prince occurs in II, iv, at the tavern.

[11]*The Fortunes of Falstaff*, p. 64.

It seems to me equally impossible to suppose the second part of *Henry IV* to be devoted to an atonement with justice—containing as it does the harsh rejection of Falstaff; Falstaff's hugely successful contrast between his own "youth" and the lord chief justice's perhaps admirable but still stiff, prosaic rectitude; and the treachery of Gaultree forest. There can be little of justice in a play in which Prince John of Lancaster goes unpunished while Falstaff is rejected. In fact the whole of the second part of *Henry IV* is a satire directed against injustice: injustice at Gaultree forest, no justice in Gloustershire, injustice in London at the coronation procession. Thematically, the first and second parts of *Henry IV* are satiric assessments of what Henry V will become through satiric appraisals of what he is, and of the falsities of public life.

If there was once a Hal, a carefree playboy whose acceptance of the world of the tavern in preference to the world of the court was real, he appears, and there only by report, in *Richard II*:

PERCY: My Lord, some two days since I saw the prince,
         And told him of those triumphs held at Oxford.
BOLING: And what said the gallant?
PERCY: His answer was, he would unto the stews,
         And from the common'st creature pluck a glove
         And wear it as a favour; and with that
         He would unhorse the lustiest challenger.

                                        (V, iii.)

A reply hardly devoid of wit, and, in its contempt for chivalry, much in the spirit of Falstaff. Yet as the prince's first soliloquy so amply demonstrates, by the opening of the first part of *Henry IV* the tavern is only a mask—as the honor of his slain "factor" Hotspur is but a mask. Indeed, the prince, with Poins in *2 Henry IV,* is nearly reminiscent of Richard II in the hauteur of his royal pretense:

PRINCE: Before God, I am exceeding weary.
POINS: Is't come to that: I had thought weariness durst not
         have attack'd one of so high blood.

PRINCE: Faith, it does me, though it discolours the complexion of
          of my greatness to acknowledge it.   (II, ii.)

A banal enough conversation, we feel, ending as it does in a
discussion of beer; but the tone anticipates another and more
serious remark—Henry's before Agincourt: "But if it be a sin
to covet honour/ I am the most offending soul alive." (*Henry
V*, IV, iii.) We remember that "honour" is Falstaff's word,
couched in a meditation induced by his glance at the dead face
of Sir Walter Blunt; we remember also, in the rhetoric of the
king before battle, the first promise of the prince: "I'll so
offend, to make offense a skill/ Redeeming time when men least
think I will." (*1 Henry IV*, I, ii.)

   This is the great irony of Henry V, prince and king; he, the
deceiver of all, deceives most of all himself. He thought to
make offense his skill, to refine offense to an art—at Agincourt,
and at Harfleur he is successful. But his "offense" is Hotspur's,
without stammar or charm, and Sir Walter Blunt's, without
the rigid grin of death. Yet Agincourt is, in its way, a masque
of death—as Henry V had solemnly told his archbishop.

   Stung at court by the Dauphin's gift of tennis balls, Henry
V begins with icy control, "We are glad the Dauphin is so
pleasant with us," but then is swept, by the torrential pouring
of his words, into images of terrifying ferocity:

             . . . for many a thousand widows,
        Shall this his mock mock out of their dear husbands,
        Mock mothers from their sons, mock castles down;
        And some are yet ungotten and unborn
        That shall have cause to curse the Dauphin's scorn.
                                        (*Henry V*, I, ii.)

Before the parley at Harfleur, Henry urges his soldiers to "imitate the actions of the tiger" (*Henry V*, III, ii); and as he
addresses the citizens of Harfleur the images of rapine which he
evokes are, like his tennis-ball speech, the fulfillment of Henry
IV's prophecy of a time when "rage and hot blood are his
counsellors":

> Therefore, you men of Harfleur,
> Take pity of your town and of your people,
> Whiles yet my soldiers are in my command,
> Whiles yet the cool and temperate wind of grace
> O'er blows the filthy and contagious clouds,
> Of heady murder, spoil, and villainy,
> If not, why in a moment look to see
> The blind and bloody soldier
> With foul hand
> Defile the locks of your shrill-shrieking daughters;
> Your fathers taken by the silver beards,
> And their most reverend heads dashed to the walls.
> Your naked infants spitted on pikes
> Whiles the mad mothers with their howls confus'd
> Do break the clouds, as did the wives of Jewry
> At Herod's bloody-hunting slaughterness.
>   (*Henry V*, III, iv.)

Henry, once the union of Machiavelli's fox and lion, is here only the lion: ferocious, raging, delighting, as did Hotspur once, in violence for its own sake. With Falstaff, Henry rejected his own humanity; in the acceptance of his father's deathbed advice, ". . . be it thy course to busy giddy minds/ With foreign quarrels . . ." (*2 Henry IV*, IV, v), there is neat conjunction of policy and disposition. Henry V is the lion run riot—a king who has transported overseas not the criminal or the crime but the state. His only animating principle is acquisitive violence.

Yet he is still, like the fox, disguised. Having purchased the fair words of that remarkable priest, the Archbishop of Canterbury whose sole theological reflection is that "miracles are ceased" (*Henry V*, I, i), Henry listens, one hopes with more patience than his audience, to an exposition of the Salique law.[12]

---

[12]Palmer's analysis of this scene is modern criticism at its best: "This archbishop certainly knows his business. The King wishes to make war; the Archbishop assures him that it is right and just for him to do so and offers him a mighty sum as insurance against the risk of losing an even mightier sum if the King should remain at peace. The king is anxious to believe that everything will go well in his absence; the Archbishop comforts his sovereign with an idyllic description of honey-bees in midsummer. He thus fulfills to perfection the traditional function of a good churchman, making it possible for his sovereign to do what he has already decided to do with a quiet mind and with the concurrence of Almighty God." (*Characters of Shakespeare*, p. 224.)

The claim having been pronounced by the archbishop "as clear as is the summer sun," the king is constrained to inquire rhetorically, "May I with right and conscience make this claim?" (*Henry V*, I, i.) Having bought this speech from his perhaps not unwilling bishops, he is at pains to shift the burden of his specious claim from his own shoulders to the archbishop's in a public gesture, couched in the strictest piety:[13]

> And God forbid, my dear and faithful lord,
> That you should fashion, wrest, or bow your reading,
> Or nicely charge your understanding soul
> With opening titles miscreate, whose right
> Suits not in native colours with the truth;
> For God doth know how many now in health
> Shall drop their blood in approbation
> Of what your reverence shall incite us to.
> Therefore take heed how you impawn our person,
> How you awake our sleeping sword of war.
> We charge you, in the name of God, take heed;
> For never two such kingdoms did contend
> Without much fall of blood; whose guiltless drops
> Are every one a woe, a sore complaint
> 'Gainst him whose wrong gives edge unto the swords
> That make such waste in brief mortality.
> Under this conjuration speak, my lord;
> For we will hear, note, and believe in heart
> That what you speak is in your conscience wash'd
> As pure as sin with baptism.
>   (*Henry V*, I, ii.)

But guilt for Henry's French war—simply an extension of his father's plan to export civil war to the Holy Land, moved by Henry V to a closer shore—is too great a burden for the king to shift. On the eve of Agincourt, again (or still) disguised,

---

[13]The reader should note the contrary opinion of Wilson Knight: "King Henry is a deeply religious man, phrase after phrase showing his reliance on God. He will not fight until his claims on France are sanctioned in terms of 'law' and 'right' by the Archbishop of Canterbury, to whose legal scholarships he appeals . . . with a stern warning that no prevarication be allowed to twist the truth in a matter so likely to invoke grievous sufferings: never does he forget those." (*The Sovereign Flower*, p. 38.)

Henry walks among his solders—testing their loyalty, as **Richard III** was tempted to do before the battle of Bosworth Field. "Methinks," remarks Henry V with remarkable complacency, "I could not die anywhere so contented as in this king's company, his cause being just and his quarrel honorable." (*Henry V*, IV, i.) The reply of the soldier Michael Williams is startling, and penetrates to the heart of the play:

But if the cause be not good, the King himself hath a heavy reckoning to make, when all those legs and arms and heads, chopp'd off in a battle, shall join together at the latter day and cry all, "We died at such a place"; some swearing, some crying for a surgeon, some upon their wives left poor behind them, some upon the debts they owe, some upon their children rawly left. I am afeared there are few die well that die in a battle; for how can they charitably dispose of anything, when blood is their argument? Now, if these men do not die well, it will be a black matter for the King that led them to it; who to disobey were against all proportion of subjection.

(*Henry V,* IV, i.)

The king answers only the last of Williams' plaints, and misconstrues what he does answer; Williams has spoken of war, but in response Henry introduces only a concept of grace not here at issue. The king's reply is no less sophistry than was the archbishop's explication of the law Salique. The lion before Harfleur, but the fox before Agincourt with his soldiers. The portrait of the king is not a pleasant one.

Harfleur's besieging lion had only threatened; now at Agincourt he acts: "The French have reinforc'd their scatter'd men/ Then every soldier kill his prisoners/ Give the word through." (*Henry V*, IV, vi.) About this, Gower has much to say: " 'Tis certain there's not a boy left alive; and the cowardly rascals that ran from the battle ha' done this slaughter. Besides, they have burned and carried away all that was in the King's tent; wherefore the King, most worthily, hath caus'd every soldier to cut his prisoner's throats. O, 'tis a gallant king." (*Henry V,* IV, vii.)

A gallant king, perhaps, but surely a ferocious one: as the king, goaded by tennis balls, had earlier promised, the wives

and mothers of France have much to mourn. Completing a
comparison between Henry V and "Alexander the Pig"—which
is, as it occurs between two massacres, assuredly a pointed comparison, Fluellen says: "As Alexander kill'd his friend Cleitus,
being in his ales and his cups; so also Harry Monmouth, being
in his right wits and his good judgments, turn'd away the fat
knight with the great belly doublet. He was full of jests, and
gipes, and knaveries, and mocks; I have forgot his name."
(*Henry V*, IV, vii.) Fluellen has forgotten Falstaff's name;
Henry V has forgotten Falstaff's spirit:

> I was not angry since I came to France
> Until this instant. Take a trumpet, herald;
> Ride thou unto the horsemen on yond hill.
> If they will fight with us, bid them come down,
> Or void the field; they do offend our sight.
> If they'll do neither, we will come to them
> And make them skirr away, as swift as stones
> Enforced from the old Assyrian slings.
> Besides, we'll cut the throats of those we have,
> And not a man of them that we shall take
> Shall taste our mercy. Go and tell them so.
>
> (*Henry V*, IV, vii.)

Henry's rage is murderous, and here unchecked. And surely it
is no accident of dramatic emphasis that he orders prisoners
slaughtered just before the Fluellen-Gower interlude, and repeats
—or amplfies—his order immediately afterward.[14] The spirit
of Falstaff ("But, I prithee, sweet wag, shall there be gallows
standing in England when thou art king?" (*1 Henry IV*, I, ii)
is as dead as the French prisoners; the only remnant of Falstaff
left in Henry V is that grim, perverted humor which leads him
to trick Cambridge, Scroop, and Grey into forswearing mercy
before their writs of execution are served.

Only the wooing of Katharine remains—a cumbersome,
clumsy scene, through which the politician shines constantly but

[14]For the judgments rendered here on Henry V before and in battle,
I am in large measure indebted to Goddard's essay on this king in *The
Meaning of Shakespeare,* pp. 237–60.

the lover never.[15] Placed beside Richard's wooing of Anne, or even Suffolk's by proxy of Margaret, Henry's courtship is devoid not only of sincerity but of grace and gallantry; its consummation is as political as its issue was to be pitiable. "I am content; so the maiden cities you talk of may wait on her; so the maid that stood in the way for my wish shall show me the way to my will." (*Henry V*, V, ii.) The results of the marriage are to be mad Henry VI, under whom ill-got France was lost, and the Wars of the Roses. From its inception the marriage was as barren of good issue as was Henry V's French war—upon the consequences of which Shakespeare had already spent three plays.

"So," wrote Wyndham Lewis of Shakespeare, "he accepted his kings: but with a much worse grace than is generally believed."[16] He had presented three titanic exemplars of intellect run riot: Richard III, whose doom was both his genius and nature's stamp, and whose rare capacity it was to anticipate his doom while relishing his genius; Richard II, drowned in his own superb though shrill and frantic rhetoric, anticipating his dying to the point of composing his own report of it; and Henry V, led by his innate duplicity to a polity that consisted not so much in the exercise of his father's advices as in the exercise of that combination of crudity and ferocity which the banishment of human feeling dictates.[17] At bottom all Shakespeare's kings—whether like Richard III and Henry IV they sought the crown with murder, or like Henry V sought it with policy and in Commodity's spirit, or like Henry VI acquired it with their swaddling clothes and never threw it off or wore it

---

[15]Palmer: "His [Henry V's] bluff but very competent wooing of Katharine, in which the word 'love' falls so easily from his lips, provokes in us the reflection that in the whole course of his long career we have never been able to detect in him one spark of disinterested affection for a living soul." (*Characters of Shakespeare*, pp. 246–47.)

[16]*The Lion and the Fox*, p. 165.

[17]It is interesting, I think, to note how completely, in his eagerness to divorce Henry V from Prince Hal, Tillyard violates his own conception of the tetralogy: ". . . *Henry V* is as truly separated from the two parts of *Henry IV* as *Richard II* is allied to them." (*Shakespeare's History Plays*, p. 309.)

comfortably—were destroyed by the fact and the burdens of royalty.

And that is the lesson of the histories for the student of Shakespearean tragedy. As to the Greeks and to Lord Acton, so to Shakespeare: power coarsens, weakens, corrupts, and renders prideful. Henry V wore the robes of power well, even— when those robes were armor—with fierce grandeur; Richard II pulled his robes around him and cried for God; Henry VI merely sat upon a dungheap. In each of the kings—whether Henry V rebuked by Williams, Richard III in terror wanting to skulk in the tents of his armies, or Henry IV uttering a last, intensely political gasp—there is a discernible gap, as in all men but especially in the great, between the perceived and the real. To credit Henry V in his public appearances as genuine or pious is to be deceived, and deceived by an author whose grasp of dramatic technique had grown much since Richard III masked his purposes between bishops, or since Richard II called for angels. Henry V has all Richard III's ferocity, but none of his charm; while Richard III observed himself, the observation of Henry V calls for a far more sophisticated technique.[18] Henry, prince and king, is curiously unmoved by the authority with which he is surrounded: Falstaff, the lord chief justice, his father. Yet each leaves a pernicious legacy,

[18]We note that the character of Henry V makes Reese uneasy: "In Henry V we find most of the right qualities. He is a natural leader, brave, disciplined and dedicated, neither greedy for power nor frightened of it. But he is not perfect. Even without looking too closely behind the bright facade, we sense something lacking in this too-flawless man. Perhaps it is Henry VI's real feeling of kinship with the peasant; or Cade's uninhibited vitality; or the limitless human understanding possessed by the Falstaff whom he banished. Shakespeare's final conception of the public figure demanded qualities to which all these men contributed: Henry V's leadership and dedication, his father's anxious stewardship, the personal piety of Henry VI, the uncomplicated patriotism of Faulconbridge, Richard II's instinctive grasp of the mystical element in kingship, Richard III's driving-force, perhaps even the earthiness of Cade. From this composite figure there emerges a vision of power rightly held and rightly administered that tells us what Shakespeare believed majesty to be." (*The Cease of Majesty*, p. 144.)

Of this we must observe that the component parts of this "vision," like abstractions in reduction division, cancel each other out.

and all three—king, judge, and jester—in spirit survive their deaths: Henry V's rhetoric is that of the lord chief justice infused with Henry's native duplicity; his statecraft is his father's mixed with Henry's own lust for war; and his brutal humor is a perversion by terrible cruelty of Falstaff's joy.

The legacy of authority tested against the aspirations of the young, then, will be one of the great Shakespearean themes; the survival of the spirit of the fathers in the sons will be another. The struggle to liberate the hero from the strictures of legacy, position, and will to power and advance him into the realm of self-discovery will be the poet's aim, achieved at last and sublimely in *Macbeth* and *King Lear*. And by 1600 Shakespeare, who had in nine great historical plays applied method to legend and made drama from historical propaganda, was uniquely well equipped with ". . . a perception, not only of the pastness of the past, but of its presence."[19]

But Shakespeare did not, as Eliot suggests, acquire his history from Plutarch; he acquired his sense of the past by distilling the history of his country into pageants, and battles, and meditations. And he learned from history that pageant or victory or conquest without realization of consequences is experience unassimilated, unused, unabsorbed—a recognition that renders *Richard III* a tragedy, and *Henry V,* as the full title implies, simply a "life." For Richard of Gloucester, at the end a self-realized man whose life and crimes have wheeled full circle against him, would trade his kingdom for a horse, and fight on; Henry V, in contrast, ends engaged in crude barter and pedantic insistence upon mere titles.

[19]Eliot, p. 268.

VII ❧ The Patrician and the Prince
Julius Caesar and *Hamlet*

TO this point we have concentrated our attention upon those of Shakespeare's English plays in which the poet was constrained by facts which, through the burden of historical truths and beliefs, or the traditions of previous drama, were familiar to his audience. That usurpers stole thrones, that dynasties flourished, warred, and died, that rulers betrayed their country and nobles betrayed their rulers were facts which Shakespeare could manipulate but not avoid. From these facts he drew lessons, and in his progress as writer and thinker from *Henry VI* to *Henry V* he developed that peculiar, retrospective view through which the victory at Agincourt is, in *Henry V,* really defeat, both moral and spiritual.

Just as "much of the weakness of Hamlet criticism has come from our tendency, so difficult to avoid, to view parts of the play on the basis of a knowledge of the whole which the Elizabethan theatre audience could not have had,"[1] so, we must insist, a great part of the difficulty which has plagued the criticism of the history plays lies precisely in neglecting the importance of, very simply, what came first. Just as the Elizabethan audience "viewing the first act [of *Hamlet*] has no reason to doubt either his [Claudius'] goodness or the accuracy

[1] Ribner, *Patterns,* p. 70.

of his description of Hamlet's condition,"[2] so we may not presume that the Elizabethan audience, schooled by the *Henry VI*
plays in the nature and scope of the national disaster which
was the legacy of Henry V, had any reason to question the
coarseness or the brutality of the ruler who rejected his friend
and attempted to solve civil war by exporting it to France.

The French witch Joan, the French whore Margaret, contentious nobles without allegiances save to self, and the prevailing anarchy which the nobles of Henry VI with their low-
life counterpart Cade represent, could have prepared the Elizabethan, and should prepare us, for the singularly unpleasant
rendering of the character and motives of the king presented in
The Life of Henry the Fifth. One may not, as Ribner properly
insists, anticipate the character of the efficient and surely regal
Claudius from a previous reading, any more than one might at
the outset glean the character of Claudius from the sullen
demeanor of his nephew; likewise we must, if we are to read
the history plays correctly, draw our conclusions from them as
they were presented. No one would contend that the three parts
of *Henry VI* were not written before *Henry V*; it seems vain,
then, to argue that the portrait of the conqueror of France was
drawn without recollection of, and reflection upon, the bitter
fruit of his conquest. Therefore, having explored the character
of the warrior in *Henry V*, we shall not be surprised to find, in
the two plays which bridge the gap between the English histories
and the mature tragedies, a demon, a "dead corse, again in
complete steel" (*Hamlet,* I, iv), and Caesar, deaf to humility
and prophecy but alive to the tumult of the mob which is as
much his creature as he is theirs.[3]

The importance of *Hamlet* and *Julius Caesar* to our study
lies not only in the essential similarity of their protagonists but
also in the fact that, while neither is a political play in the

[2]Ribner, p. 70.

[3]Goddard clarifies Shakespeare's lesson: "After the indictment of imperialism in *Henry V, Julius Caesar* is just the combined confirmation of
that indictment and compensation for it that might have been expected.
It makes plain that those who oppose imperialism with force run the
risk of being no better than the imperialists themselves." (*The Meaning
of Shakespeare,* p. 330.)

sense of the English histories, both are deeply involved with those ethical and intellectual processes in the private man which dictate the activities and reactions of the public man. *Julius Caesar* and *Hamlet* represent an enlargement of the intellectual and moral dimensions of the hero—an enlargement by virtue of which, while both Hamlet and Marcus Brutus are given an opportunity to meditate upon their course of action, neither is bound to his choice until relatively late in the play.

We ought not, as we study *Caesar* and *Hamlet,* to be troubled with contrasting political ideas; republicanism, or its restoration, is no more serious an alternative to dictatorship in Rome than is Hamlet to Claudius in Denmark. "Caesarism," Dover Wilson's "equality of all in one classless mob, united in reverence before a semi-divine being, whether Napoleon, Führer, or general secretary of the Communist party,"[4] is not here at issue, for the succession to Caesar is determined, not by the witless mob, but by the human failures of the conspirators, who, having slain Caesar, are unable to wrest his mantle from men more practical than they. Claudius and Fortinbras are very real antagonists, as Antony and Octavius are in history and in spirit Caesor's heirs; Brutus and Hamlet by contrast are men essentially apart from the events through which they move, but which they so seldom dominate. Shakespeare, in *Caesar* and *Hamlet,* is exploring not politics but ". . . the question of how men come to deliver themselves to illusion, of how they construct for themselves a world in which, because it is not the world of reality but a projection of their own, they inevitably come to disaster."[5]

And the importance of *Julious Caesar* and *Hamlet, Prince of Denmark* centers in the poet's development of the prince and the Roman patrician Brutus as men of thought and feeling whose actions are consequent not so much upon the pressures

[4]See Dover Wilson's introduction to *Julius Caesar,* particularly the section on "Caesar and Caesarism." The quotation is from p. xxx.

[5]Knights, *Further Explorations,* p. 35. Knights' discussion of Shakespeare's handling of the Roman mob, and of the mob's reaction to the activities of the participants in the political events of the play, is particularly illuminating. (Pp. 47–49.)

of events as upon those choices which drive the Roman to action and the Dane to a kind of numbed paralysis. For Brutus and Hamlet are unique, and uniquely together, in their determination not only to do the right thing, but also to discover, by logic and reflection, what the right thing is. Yet each, though among Shakespeare's political characters the most contemplative and the least self-seeking, fails. It is this process of failure, in men well meaning and well disposed, which leads us, as it led Shakespeare, to the ultimate options, one for sublime evil and one for sublime good, which the last British plays, *Macbeth* and *King Lear,* represent.

It might, for instance, be possible to take Brutus seriously as Rome's savior, had we not already seen Rome: "O you hard hearts, you cruel men of Rome,/ Knew you not Pompey?" (I, i.) As the city will later sway between allegiance to Brutus, Caesor's murderer—"Let him be Caesar," (III, ii) cries the third plebeian—and Antony, so the mob that once loved Pompey now loves Caesar.[6] That the republic is long since dead is apparent in the play's opening; our attention is turned, with quick and brutal immediacy, to the question of who shall succeed Caesar—for, like Elizabeth, Caesar's Calpurnia is barren. And Rome is nearly as filled with murderers as with hero-worshipers; but of two sorts only. Cassius is afraid, and envious; Brutus, not only withdrawn from public life but also the prisoner of ideas which have lost both truth and relevance, is a reactionary recluse.[7] Cassius dreams of greatness, Brutus of the republic; but in their dreams only once does either touch reality—when Brutus, in his orchard, cries, "O that we then could come by Caesar's spirit/ And not dismember Caesar." (II, i.)

If there is a political lesson in *Julius Caesar,* it is that the spirit of tyranny survives the tyrant—to the point of forcing

[6]Ribner's view of Caesar is similar to the one presented here: "It is wrong to regard *Julius Caesar* as a play about a king who is murdered by rebellious citizens. It is a play about a great general who aspires to be a king and who is murdered on the eve of his success." (P. 54.)

[7]Palmer offers a different word for Brutus, which implies a differing view: "Brutus has precisely the qualities which in every age have rendered the conscientious liberal ineffectual in public life." (*Political Characters,* p. 1.)

the would-be liberator to require from Cassius the money that
his scruples will not permit him to raise himself:

> I did send to you
> For certain sums of gold, which you deni'd me;
> For I can raise no money by vile means.
> By heaven, I had rather coin my heart
> And drop my blood for drachmas than to wring
> From the hard hands of peasants their vile trash
> By any indirections—I did send
> To you for gold to pay my legions
> Which you deni'd me.   (IV, iii.)

There is, in all of *Julius Caesar,* no more singular instance of
the patrician cast of Brutus' thought than this. He will not
bleed peasants, but he needs money; so Cassius, Cassius the
coarse, must provide it.[8]

Yet there was a time when this same Cassius sang sweetly
into the ear of Marcus Brutus, when he talked of tradition, of
family, of the old Rome. Like Hamlet before the appearance of
his father's ghost, Brutus has been troubled:

> Vexed I am
> With passions of some difference,
> Conceptions only proper to myself,
> Which give some soil perhaps to my behaviours . . .
>
>   (I, ii.)

Portia tells us that he does not sleep; and she insists, to Brutus,
"You have some sick offence within your mind." (II, i.) Bru-
tus' illness is that he cannot bend, either to the mob or to its
Caesar; unable to stoop, he will murder. "Honor," Cassius
tells Brutus as he tempts him, "is the subject of my story." (I, ii.)
"Honor," Falstaff's word—but it is not honor, only the spirit

---

[8]Goddard rightly regards this as the second of Brutus' torturing of
logic: "He will not wring gold from the peasants by an indirection. But
he will take it, even demand it, of Cassius, who, of course, has no other
ultimate source from which to obtain it than just those peasants. Brutus
is doing what in the same breath he declares he would rather die than
do." (*The Meaning of Shakespeare,* p. 325.)

of the fathers, which Cassius, knowing his patrician auditor as
well as Antony will later know the mob, invokes:

> O, you and I have heard our fathers say
> There was a Brutus once that would have brook'd
> Th' eternal devil to keep his state in Rome
> As easily as a king.   (I, ii.)[9]

Brutus, disturbed before and warped further by Cassius'
conjurings of what once was and what might be, pauses to
reflect. And it is Shakespeare's comment upon the faithful sons
of the fathers that Brutus thinks as badly as he acts; he sees no
fault in Caesar, but fears one; finding no grounds for the
murderous act upon which he is now very nearly determined,
he abandons thought and construes events to suit:

> And, since the quarrel
> Will bear no colour for the thing he is,
> Fashion it thus: that what he is, augmented,
> Would run to these and these extremities:
> And therefore think him as a serpent's egg
> Which, hatch'd, would, as his mind, grow
>   mischievous,
> And kill him in the shell.   (II, i.)

The decision to murder Caesar for faults imagined because
these faults are not present is the abandonment of thought upon
which *Julius Caesar* depends.[10] To this point Brutus the Stoic

[9]Of this passage Goddard writes, "Cassius knows his brother will en-
tertain no proposal save for the general good. So he attacks him where
virtue and its opposite are forever getting confused, in his pride, pride
in his ancestors' dedication to republicanism . . . the fathers once more!
It is the clinching argument. Brutus capitulates to the past, or rather
to Cassius' subtle perversion of it (the earlier Brutus did not kill the tyrant)." (*The Meaning of Shakespeare*, p. 314.)

[10]This—Brutus' orchard speech—is the critical moment in *Julius
Ceasar*. Knights, whose essay, like my own, reflects his indebtedness to the
insights of Goddard, describes Brutus' soliloquy as having "the air of tortuous unreality . . ." (*Further Explorations*, p. 41.) Richmond's analysis
is particularly devastating: "no system of justice has ever yet succeeded
in effectively evaluating criminal intent—particularly when, as in this case,
the prosecutor cannot even bring in circumstantial evidence, because he
still lacks the perception to recognize that his own hypothesis of Caesar's
manic tyranny has already been realized in all but title." (*Shakespeare*,
p. 207.) For a contrasting view, see Ribner's analysis in *Patterns*, p. 55ff.

was free, if troubled; from this point forward he is tradition's creature. Cassius throws him letters purporting to be from the citizens whom Caesar and Antony—but not Brutus—know so well, and it is a measure of the illusions among which Marcus Brutus now dwells that these false letters prompt him to familial retrospection rather than thought: "My ancestors did from the streets of Rome/ The Tarquin drive when he was call'd a king." (II, i.) With the devotion of old, ill Caius Ligarius, Brutus is the slave of a duty that is no duty at all; to Ligarius "it sufficeth/ That Brutus leads me on." (II, i.)

The errors of Brutus, as he moves from the darkness of his garden to the darkness at Phillipi, are both legion and legend. No man dies but Caesar, and Antony prevails. Brutus permits Antony to speak to the mob, and Antony, by playing again upon Falstaff's word "honor,"[11] brings the mob to that memorable ferocity in which the citizens of Rome tear Cinna for his verses.[12] It remains only for Brutus to bring his army, as he has brought himself, from the heights to the depths of Phillipi, where both army and Brutus are defeated.

Ensnared by the echoes of a dead past, Brutus is Shakespeare's first great lesson in that ethical failure which proceeds from the distortion or abandonment of thought. For Brutus was not, as the English kings were, the victim of circumstances. He and greatness were not compelled to kiss, as greatness and Henry Bolingbroke were in part; Brutus murdered because he imagined the future, instead of realizing the present.

The Prince of Denmark is no less troubled, when first we meet him, than was Marcus Brutus; that Brutus meditates upon murder and Hamlet upon suicide is a difference more in degree than in kind. The fundamental similarity between the two plays is that both the Dane and the Roman are destroyed by that failure of the intellect which proceeds from acceptance of the spirit of the fathers. The ghost of Hamlet's father and the

[11]See Wilson Knight's superb analysis of the word honor, and the perspectives from which Brutus, Antony, and Cassius view both the word and the idea, in *The Imperial Theme*.

[12]In treating this brutal episode Richmond brilliantly validates the contentions of his preface: "this scene is a Hobbesian vision of human nature, if ever there was one . . ." (*Political Plays*, p. 209.)

ancestors of Marcus Brutus are the obstacles over which both prince and patrician stumble.[13]

We have seen that Brutus is impelled to action by a tradition which has no relevance to his circumstances, for Caesar is no Tarquin and the people of Rome are not citizens but slaves—and slaves who change masters with a ready will. Similarly, Hamlet, at thirty part philosopher and in very large part arrested adolescent, is so swayed by his father's apparition that his intellect, no more disciplined and of no greater effect than that of Brutus, deserts him. At each of the crises of his life-journey, Hamlet fails: Ophelia sickens and dies; Polonius, in a rage mistaken for Claudius, is murdered; and at the end the prince's objective—the death of Claudius, whom he would not execute as Claudius prayed—is accomplished by stratagems not of Hamlet's devising.[14]

Hamlet's fault, like Brutus', is intellectual; he tests not the Ghost, but the king:

> I'll have these players
> Play something like the murder of my father
> Before mine Uncle. I'll observe his looks;
> I'll tent him to the quick. If he but blench,
> I know my course. The spirit that I have seen
> May be the devil; and the devil hath power
> T'assume a pleasing shape; yea, and perhaps
> Out of my weakness and my melancholy,
> As he is very potent with such spirits,
> Abuses me to damn me. I'll have grounds
> More relative than this. The play's the thing
> Wherein I'll catch the conscience of the king.
>   (II, ii.)

[13]Goddard: ". . . let us see what is involved in the assumption that Shakespeare thought it was Hamlet's duty to kill the King. It involves nothing less than the retraction of all the Histories, of *Romeo and Juliet*, and *Julius Caesar*." (*The Meaning of Shakespeare*, p. 336.)

[14]So dismal a rendering of Hamlet's failures may, I hope, serve to weaken the picture of the prince which Dover Wilson imagines: ". . . a great, an almost superhuman, figure tottering beneath a tragic burden too heavy even for his mighty back; or, if you will, of a genius suffering from a total weakness and battling against it, until in the end it involves him in the catastrophe which is at once his liberation and atonement." (*What happens in Hamlet*, p. 237.)

This is the moment of Hamlet's failure. Until this time, even haunted, bitter, and obsessed, he has been free to choose; here he determines to test only the Ghost's veracity, not its origin or the morality of its prompting.[15] And he hopes to find the truth of the Ghost reflected in the darkest of all the recesses in *Hamlet*—the mirror of the conscience of Claudius. From this point, Hamlet is a character trapped by his own faulty intellection no less surely than was Marcus Brutus trapped when he sought to justify Caesar's murder by imagining Caesar's future crimes.

And—lest we miss the point—Laertes and Ophelia are doomed by the spirit of fidelity to a father notably less impressive than is the incarnation of the elder Hamlet.[16] At that moment in which Ophelia obeys her father, she defiles her love; her reply to Polonius, "I shall obey, my lord" (I, iii), is as piteous as her last mad, sad songs.[17] And when Laertes is driven, by the promptings of Claudius and his own hatred for Hamlet, to a stratagem which serves only to show the growing desperation of the King of Denmark, who at the outset rules uneasily but well, the lesson Shakespeare intended—the ignoble acts which proceed from perversion of thought by emotions and affections intensified in retrospect—is completed. Hamlet is

[15]The theological nature of the ghost of the elder Hamlet is best stated, I think, by Lily B. Campbell: "I truly believe that if a Papist and King James and Timothy Bright had seen the play, as they all probably did, each would have gone home confirmed in his own opinion about ghosts." (*Shakespeare's Heroes*, p. 128.) Dover Wilson's discussion of the Ghost (*What Happens in Hamlet*, pp. 52–86) is, as always, interesting, but his own liability to what is here described as Hamlet's error in discernment is surely clear: ". . . obdurate Protestants would refuse to admit him [the Ghost] as anything but a devil even after the play scene had proved the truth of his story . . ."
   It is at least clear that the Ghost, which Goddard describes as "the spirit of war itself," complains of the warmth of his lodging.

[16]For an interesting and clear discussion of this structuring, see Campbell's *Shakespeare's Heroes*, pp. 109ff.

[17]"Who can doubt—what juxtaposition Shakespeare achieves!—that this scene was written to be placed just before the one between Hamlet and the Ghost? There another father pours poison of another kind into the ear of a son as innocent in his way as Ophelia was in hers. The temptation this time is not to sensuality under the name of purity but to violence under the name of honor." (Goddard, p. 352.)

destroyed, Ophelia maddened, and Laertes rendered no more than an assassin by the initial, unthinking fidelity of each to authority they ought to have rejected.

Revenge is no more moral than the Ghost is good, and Hamlet the philosopher falls victim to the defects of his own processes of thought.[18] He, like Brutus, and like Laertes and Ophelia, is betrayed by tradition and the spirit of the fathers.

But at last the Ghost is denied, for Fortinbras, the son of that King of Norway whom the elder Hamlet defeated, will rule in Denmark. As for Marcus Brutus, his murderous exertions serve only to mature, in Antony and Octavian, that remorseless tyranny which Brutus feared—but in Caesar, only imagined. So Shakespeare's last commentary upon these, his great, trapped characters, is that they unwittingly brought into being what tradition and the spirit of the fathers would have taught them most to despise: the Roman Empire and the Norwegian conquest.

[18]For a differing, and fascinating, interpretation see Ribner's essay on *Hamlet*. Ribner contends that "in the fifth act Hamlet has submitted to the will of God . . . has no particular plan for killing Claudius, and he seems to feel no need for one. . . . The ineffective schemer of the first three acts is no more; Hamlet has become a passive instrument in the hands of divine providence. He will cleanse from Denmark the Evil of Claudius just as an earlier Richmond had freed England from the Curse of Richard III." (*Patterns*, pp. 89–91.)

The great strength of Ribner's interpretation lies not only in the force and brilliance with which it is presented, but also in that—if the Christian bias is admitted—Hamlet's terminal paralysis is made both plausible and dramatically functional. But in Gunnar Boklund's "Judgment in *Hamlet*" the idea of Hamlet's being at last submissive to God is objected to both with humor and considerable force: "Without claiming much knowledge of what submission to God should mean, I must, however, point out the basic weakness of this [Ribner's] interpretation. One should, as far as I can see, submit to God's will with joy, satisfaction, or at least a positive conviction, and there is no sign of this in Hamlet." (P. 133.)

We might add that not even through the most tortuous of orthodox constructions may we accept the notion that Gertrude owed God a death.

VIII ❧ Damnation and Transfiguration
Macbeth and *King Lear*

I T was not until the years 1605 and 1606 that Shakespeare, having since 1599 wandered among the writings of Saxo Grammaticus, Plutarch, and Cinthio for his plots and having rendered the Dane, the Roman, and the Venetian both superbly and superbly Elizabethan, returned to the stories of the Island Kingdoms and their rulers. He may have turned back to the theme of monarchy because of his interest in the new reign, but it is most important for our study to realize what depth and completion the combination of *Macbeth* and *King Lear*, both written in little more than a year, add to Shakespeare's portrayal of rulers, only kings when he began in the 1590s but now heroes.

By 1605 Shakespeare had written twenty-seven plays, among which were nine histories and five tragedies; he thus brought to the writing of *Macbeth* and *King Lear* a wealth of historical and political insight unrivaled before or since in the English theater, and also an awareness of human impulsion which had never ceased to deepen after Somerset and Plantagenet, in adolescent fury, plucked roses in *1 Henry VI*. His success assured but his life by its records no happier than most, Shakespeare was able to write in *Macbeth* about the mature—their passions and frustrations—and in *King Lear* about the glory which may attend great age; he was able as well to present in the first of these two great tragedies the fascination of ultimate evil, and in the second a secular vision of transfiguration.[1]

Among the most fundamental aspects of Macbeth is his crudity; at the last his rhetoric soars above it, but crudity marks and mars him throughout.[2] Of all Shakespeare's creations Macbeth is the most elemental; he is close to the earth, violence is native to him, and the witches whose coarse rhymes pluck his thoughts to the crown are no less an upwelling of the primitive than is Macbeth himself.[3] Violence is his duty, and his pleasure:

[1]As I followed Sisson's dating of *King John* and *Richard II*, I shall also follow his dating of *Macbeth* and *King Lear*. Of *Macbeth*, Sisson wrote, "It seems reasonable to place it in the year preceding *King Lear*, i.e., in 1605." (*Shakespeare*, p. 969.) The reader ought, however, to be familiar with objections to this dating: Ribner regards the writing of *Macbeth* in 1606 and its performance at court on August 7 of that year as "virtually certain." (*Patterns*, p. 153.) Kenneth Muir, in his introduction to the Arden *Macbeth* (p. 50), contends that "Macbeth . . . was first performed in the year 1606; that is to say, it comes after *Hamlet, Othello, Measure for Measure,* and *King Lear,* and *Cleopatra* and *Coriolanus.*"

Perhaps the most imaginative dating of *Macbeth* is Dover Wilson's; admittedly guessing, Wilson wonders whether Shakespeare did not perhaps write *Macbeth* for a court performance at Edinburgh before the death of Elizabeth, and then later compress it for a performance in 1606 before James and Christian of Denmark. (See Wilson's introduction to *Macbeth*, pp. 39–42.)

[2]Campbell notices, although she does not emphasize, Macbeth's essential bestiality: "The Macbeth here [V, vii] is the Macbeth of the first scenes of the play, the Macbeth in military action, the Macbeth who recalls the 'brave Macbeth' with whom the play opened. But here again he fights irrationally, not with the fortitude of the man controlling his passion by reason, but rather with the courage of the animal that fights without reason when there is no choice but to fight for its life. Shakespeare could not say any more clearly that this apparent courage is that of the beast and not the man." (*Shakespeare's Heroes*, pp. 236–67.)

Campbell is most rewarding when considering the plays themselves, but less so when discussing their sources. Her notion, for instance, "that Shakespeare patterned his study upon the edicts of the philosophers in their anatomies of the passions here studied seems obvious" (p. 212) is in point of fact not obvious at all. *Macbeth* is far more—as Campbell herself recognizes when she departs from her absolute values—than a study of "rash courage and fear" (p. 238).

[3]The reader should note the contrary view; my conception of Macbeth as a brute from the play's opening is one which Ribner does not share: "On the disintegration of Macbeth the man, Shakespeare lavishes his principal attention. He is careful to paint his hero in the opening scenes as

> . . . brave Macbeth—well he deserves that name—
> Disdaining Fortune, with his brandish'd steel,
> Which smok'd with bloody execution,
> Like Valour's minion carv'd out his passage
> Till he fac'd the slave;
> Which ne'er shook hands, nor bade farewell to him,
> Till he unseam'd him from the nave to th' chaps,
> And fix'd his head upon our battlements.
>
> (I, i.)

The spirit of this bloody man, the personification of war, partakes of the servant. His familiars the witches have masters;[4] so ought Macbeth, and he knows it: "He [Duncan] hath honour'd me of late; and I have bought/ Golden opinions from all sorts of people . . ." (I, vii.) Indeed, the breathless letter from Cawdor's new thane to his lady is, in its eloquence and in the rush of its description, disruptive; Macbeth's asides to this point, harsh and pithy, are as paradoxical as cryptic:

> My thought, whose murder yet is but fantastical,
> Shakes so my single state of man that function
> Is smother'd in surmise, and nothing is
> But what is not.   (I, iii.)

Macbeth's rhetoric—to the witches or to the lords of Scotland— is as sharply differentiated from Banquo's measured eloquence as is the naiveté of Duncan's "There's no art/ To find the mind's construction in the face" (I, iv) from Macbeth's later, ironic, and hugely accurate "Your spirits shine through you" to Banquo's murderers. (III, i.) Banquo and Duncan, perfect thane and perfect king, are too good for the world and will shortly leave it; Macbeth, more himself with witches and murderers

a man of great stature, 'full of the milk of human kindness.' " (*Patterns,* p. 165.) On the same subject and in a similar vein, Dover Wilson slips, all unaware, into precisely that rhetoric which Falstaff debunked at Shrewsbury: "Macbeth was no criminal to start with, but an honorable soldier . . ." (*Macbeth,* Introduction, p. 59.)

[4]The essentially servile nature of the witches is one which Bradley is at some pains to press: "His [Shakespeare's] witches owe all their power to the spirits; they are '*instruments* of darkness'; the spirits are their 'masters.' Fancy the fates having masters!" (*Shakespearean Tragedy,* p. 273.)

than with his wife, is the servant mentality run amok.[5] His
robes sit no more easily upon him than does the ass's head upon
Bottom, for each is at the outset a gross vessel.[6] And lest Macbeth's kinship with the base be missed, the dominant symbolic
pattern of the play is a pervasive animalism: "I dare do all
that may become a man," responds Macbeth to his wife's reproaches, and he adds pointedly, "Who dares [do] more is none."
His wife in reply seizes upon Macbeth's own image:

> What beast was't, then,
> That made you break this enterprise to me?
> When you durst do it, then you were a man;
> And, to be more than what you were, you would
> Be so much more the man.   (I, vii.)

And the image—the ironic inversion of those acts which become
men as opposed to those which become beasts—is completed in
Macbeth's stricture to his wife, "Bring forth men-children only
. . ." (I, vii). For Macbeth's acts, from the dagger-haunted
murder of Duncan to the slaughter of Macduff's family, are a
series of bestialities. The servant kills his master; the servant,
now master, lashes about him in insensate rage. The imagaic
dichotomy between men and brutes never leaves the play:

> 1. Mur.:   We are men, my liege.
>   Macbeth: Ay, in the catalogue ye go for men,
> As hounds and greyhounds, mongrels, spaniels, curs,
> Shoughs, water-rugs, and demi-wolves are clept
> All by the name of dogs; the valued file
> Distinguishes the swift, the slow, the subtle,
> The housekeeper, the hunter, every one,

[5]This is a notion that Wilson Knight touches upon but does not pursue:
"The value of warriorship may not be associated with allegiance; it is
one with the ideal of kingship and imperial power. . . . Sons, kinsmen,
thanes—all are bound close together. Scotland is a family, Duncan its
head. A natural law binds all degrees in proper place and allegiance."
(*The Imperial Theme*, p. 126.)

[6]"On the ethical—as opposed to the metaphysical—plane, Macbeth
fails through trying to advance from deserved honour as a noble thane
to the higher kingly honour to which he has no rights. This kingship he
attains, yet he never really possesses it. He is never properly king: his
regality is a mockery." Knight, *The Imperial Theme*, p. 120.)

> According to the gift which bounteous nature
> Hath in him clos'd; whereby he does receive
> Particular addition, from the bill
> That writes them all alike; and so of men.
> Now, if you have a station in the file,
> Not i' th' worst rank of manhood, say 't;
> And I will put that business in your bosoms,
> Whose execution takes your enemy off,
> Grapples you to the heart and love of us,
> Who wear our health but sickly in his life,
> Which in his death were perfect.
>   (III, i.)

This injunction to murder, like Lady Macbeth's, is perverted; the murderers will shortly be joined in the execution of their bestial proof of manhood by the king, surely "the perfect spy o' the time" to whom he himself refers.[7] But Lady Macbeth is not done with perversions; at the banquet she attempts to recall the beast from his vision of the gory Banquo with injunctions to his manhood. "Are you a man?" she asks, and again, "What, quite unmann'd in folly?" And to the ghost, Macbeth, mixing visions of the real and the supernatural, the terrors of the flesh and of the spirit, cries out:

> What man dare, I dare.
> Approach thou like the rugged Russian bear,
> The arm'd rhinoceros, or th' Hyrcan tiger;
> Take any shape but that, and my firm nerves
> Shall never tremble. Or be alive again,
> And dare me to the desert with thy sword;

[7]The idea that Macbeth is the third of Banquo's murderers is one which Kenneth Muir dismisses, in his notes for the Arden *Macbeth* (p. 90), as "fantastic"; nonetheless, Dover Wilson, in the notes to his Cambridge edition (p. 137), makes my point for me. "I suggest," wrote Wilson, "that 5 h. adds him [the third murderer] (perhaps originally introducing him at the end of 3. 1.), to show that Macb., tyrant-like, feels he must spy even on his own chosen instruments." One is contrained to inquire who, if the tyrant must spy, would be a better spy than the tyrant himself?

Goddard notices that the third murderer is the first of the three to recognize Banquo, that he betrays familiarity with Banquo's habits, and is more disturbed than the other two by the escape of Fleance. (*The Meaning of Shakespeare*, pp. 510–11.)

> If trembling I inhabit then, protest me
> The baby of a girl. Hence, horrible shadow!
> Unreal mock'ry, hence!
>
>   [Ghost vanishes.]
>   Why, so; being gone,
> I am a man again.   (III, iv.)

To Macbeth, the most horrible image of his bestiality is
yet to come; confronted by Macduff—the news of whose unnatural birth "hath cow'd," Macbeth tells him, "my better part
of man"—the king is momentarily inert. But Macduff stirs
him to action again—by the suggestion of imprisonment as in
a zoo:

> Then yield thee, coward,
> And live to be the show and gaze o' th' time!
> We'll have thee, as our rarer monsters are,
> Painted upon a pole, and underwrit,
> "Here may you see the tyrant."
>   (V, viii.)

And at end, the head of the "bloody butcher" (V, viii) is
impaled—as, the captain tells us, the noble servant Macbeth
had earlier impaled the head of the rebel Macdonwald.

It is, then, the function of *Macbeth's* pervasive symbolism,
whether applied to kings or to murderers, to suggest that by
virtue of those acts by which men raise themselves to be more
than they are, they become less; they become beasts.[8]

The political theme in *Macbeth* is hardly, as Tillyard supposes, like the theme of *Richard III*, ". . . where likewise the
body politic asserts itself against the monstrous individual."[9] To
believe that Scotland simply disgorges Macbeth, or that Mal-

---

[8]This is a pattern of imagery which Goddard notices earlier in the
play: " 'What beast was't then,/ That made you break this enterprise to
me?' Lady Macbeth had asked long before. At last Macbeth realizes
that he is indeed slipping below even "the worst rank of manhood" to
a bestial level of 'demi-wolves' and 'hounds,' of insects, even! As the
most horrifying, and yet pathetic, line in the play reveals in the next
scene: 'O, full of scorpions is my mind, dear wife!' " (*The Meaning of
Shakespeare,* p. 507.)

[9]*Shakespeare's History Plays,* p. 317.

colm is more than an intrusive character whose function is fatuously to delineate the "King-becoming graces" in a scene rendered notable only by Macduff's grief, is to suppose that tragedy has civil philosophy as its focal point.[10] We would rather believe and have earlier noted that the sole structural distinction of significance we may make between Shakespeare's tragedies and his histories rests upon the artificial, and usually hugely unsatisfactory, political solutions to the tragedies; the critic who views Fortinbras as the solution to the problems of *Hamlet,* Octavius to the problems of *Antony and Cleopatra,* or Malcolm to the problems of *Macbeth* is a better student of government than of drama. In the tragedies, political solutions and the functional characters by which political solutions are achieved are very secondary indeed. Only in the library, never in the theatre, may one descend from the magnificence of Macbeth's meditations to the platitudes of Malcolm without a sense of acute loss.

In tragedy the focus is upon the individual, and tragedy is diminished—as *Macbeth* is diminished by the English Malcolm scene—by the displacement of that focus. The characteristic of great tragedy is the ability of the principal to dominate events upon a grand scale; *Hamlet* is a lesser play than *Macbeth* by the degree to which Hamlet is the force acted upon, rather than being himself the active force. *Macbeth,* excepting that single distortion of which Tillyard so fervently approves, is concentrated wholly upon a principal splendidly animated, splendidly dominating.

And Macbeth is a force, a servant perfect of his kind, who through communication with darker forces is moved to rise, to render the world askew by the slaughter through which he wades. He is the ultimate primitive, far more closely attuned to the powers of dark impulsion than man may safely be, and

---

[10]Surely Malcolm is not, as Ribner suggests, "Shakespeare's ideal king," nor is Macduff "a force of divine retribution generated by Macbeth's own course of evil." (*Patterns,* p. 160.) Malcolm's and Macduff's scene together is as intrusive as discursive, and it does to the keen political sensitivity of Shakespeare far too little credit to view Malcolm's paradoxical "graces"— suggesting as they do a mixture of Richard III and Henry VI at Towton— as Shakespeare's delineation of the ideal king.

at last he is emptied by complete fulfillment of those urges which no man may indulge.

The supreme instinct of the slave is to kill the master and become master himself; this Macbeth does, having with his brutal, sensual wife stilled murmurings more reflective of the servant than the servant's conscience.[11] For if Lady Macbeth knows her husband's animalism, Macbeth knows his place. And Macbeth has communed with evil; where Banquo asks, of the witches, "Whither are they vanish'd?" Macbeth cries, "Would they had stay'd!" (I, iii.) And unlike Banquo, Macbeth will seek evil again, and in the primitive's terms: he asks the witches— and these are the basic religious stirrings—for relief from present affliction and foreknowledge. Macbeth is evil's obscene priest. Lady Macbeth, more literal and less stirred by the elemental, is only the Thane of Cawdor's unsexed vestal. And because she is only worldly, she is destroyed.[12] Her husband, by contrast, perseveres to an end completely ghastly because complete.

Communion with evil, the destruction of the master, the full sexuality so richly displayed in imagery and action by the lusty thane and his lady, absolute power—these call forth the impulses that drive the primitive to whom the restrictions and laws of the folkway are but words. It is not conscience but the folkway which says, "He's here in double trust:/ First, as I am his kinsman and his subject,/ Strong both against the deed; then, as his host,/ Who should against his murderer shut the door,/ Not bear the knife myself." (I, vii.) But the folkway is overborne, and Duncan dies. After the murder of Banquo and his shade's appearance at the banquet, the new king turns, not to his queen, but to evil:

[11]Wilson Knight's observation that "warriorship and love [are] ever close in Shakespeare, either in contrast or association" (*The Imperial Theme,* p. 127), recalls scenes as diverse as the brilliant, martial Richard's wooing of Anne over a corpse and Henry V's awkward, greedy wooing of that Katharine whose France he had decimated.

[12]To Bradley's notion that Lady Macbeth was "too great to repent" (*Shakespearean Tragedy,* p. 301), we might reply that she was simply too gross.

> I will tomorrow,
> And betimes I will, to the weird sisters.
> More shall they speak; for now I am bent to know,
> By the worst means, the worst.   (III, iv.)

When Macbeth turns from his wife,[13] before this time the
repository of his hopes, griefs, and fears, if not all his murders,
he loses the dimension of sexuality. He seeks to lose fear, and
with the witches he does so—but he loses lineal hope as well.
He is now a man without a woman, a man whose tenure of
security is brief, bleak—but absolute. His power is entire, exer-
cised without restraint; his evil—the evil to which he has sur-
rendered, not an evil which possessed him—has rendered him,
now and forever alone, the perfect tyrant:

> From this moment
> The very firstlings of my heart shall be
> The firstlings of my hand.   (IV, i.)[14]

[13]Bradley fails us upon the matter of Macbeth's alienation from his
wife; "and if," he writes, "as time goes on, they drift a little apart, they
are not vulgar souls to be alienated and recriminate when they experience
the fruitlessness of their ambition." (*Shakespearean Tragedy*, p. 278.) In
fact Macbeth and his queen are totally severed, and both partake in that
spiritual desolation peculiar to their natures. But my objection is one
which Bradley himself anticipated—"Neither can I agree with those who
find in his [Macbeth's] reception of the news of his wife's death proof
of his alienation or utter carelessness." (P. 289.) Yet, in the second of
Bradley's lectures on Macbeth, he contradicts himself: "Thinking of the
change in him [Macbeth] we imagine the bond between them slackened,
and Lady Macbeth left much alone. She sinks slowly downward . . . at
last her nature, not her will, gives way." (P. 299.)

Ribner is both more succinct and more faithful to the text: ". . . as
the force of evil severs Macbeth from the rest of humanity, it also breaks
down the bond which ties him to his wife . . . This theme of family
disintegration is repeated in Macduff's desertion of his wife and children."
(*Patterns*, p. 164.)

[14]It is at this point that Bradley sees the death of Macbeth's imagination—which he has earlier described as "excitable and intense, but narrow" (p. 281)—rather than recognizing this as the instant from which
Macbeth's imagination shall be born; "the witches," Bradley wrote, "have
done their work, and after this purposeless butchery his imagination will
trouble him no more. He has dealt his last blow at the conscience and
the pity which spoke through it." (P. 288.) The significant flaw in Bradley's otherwise brilliant study of *Macbeth* is, it seems to me, his consistent
confusion of "conscience" and "imagination"—perhaps best reflected here.

Macbeth is now the union of wish, will, and action. He is as much the ultimate expression of power as its personification— the savage without restraint, prodded no longer by animalism, whole now in the grand fury which the will to do evil combined with the authority to see that evil be done engenders.

We do not see the king again for 443 lines—not until after the slaughter at Fife, the parade of Vice and Virtue in England, the presentation of his wife's madness, and the approach of his enemies to Scotland. But even in his absence his shadow is long: Malcolm retraces his crimes and the queen recites his villainies in pathetic fragments. The King of Scotland is alone.

When he reappears, he is the embodiment of whirling violence:

MACB.: The devil damn thee black,
            thou cream-fac'd loon!
        Where got'st thou that goose look?
SERV.: There is ten thousand—
MACB.:   Geese, villain?
SERV.:   Soldiers, sir.
MACB.: Go prick thy face, and over-red thy fear,
        Thou lily-liver'd boy. What soldiers,
            patch?
        Death of thy soul! those linen cheeks
            of thine
        Are counsellors to fear. What soldiers,
            whey-face?   (V, iii.)

A brutal rhetoric, as brutal as the king. But there is a new, grand dimension, and a dawning recognition:

    I have liv'd long enough. My way of life
    Is fallen into the sear, the yellow leaf;
    And that which should accompany old age,
    As honour, love, obedience, troops of friends,
    I must not look to have; but, in their stead,
    Curses, not loud but deep, mouth-honour, breath
    Which the poor heart would fain deny, and dare not.
                                           (V, iii.)

The king, now a man in whom violence and meditation are mixed almost equally, tender and ferocious by turns, is at last as ripened in horror as the autumnal cast of his rhetoric suggests. Yet he is king:

> . . . skirr the country round;
> Hang those that talk of fear. Give me mine
>   armour.
> How does your patient, doctor?   (V, iii.)

But his hopes are as hollow, as rhetorical, as his questions; his mind is as haunted as his soul is blasted.[15] Still he knows love and concern:

> Canst thou not minister to a mind diseas'd,
> Pluck from the memory a rooted sorrow,
> Raze out the written troubles of the brain,
> And with some sweet oblivious antidote
> Cleanse the stuff'd bosom of that perilous stuff
> Which weighs upon the heart?   (V, iii.)

For his wife Macbeth seeks a sweet oblivion; for himself he seeks only oblivion itself. "I have supp'd full with horrors"; then, upon hearing that the cries of the women were the knell of his wife,

> She should have died hereafter;
> There would have been a time for such a word.
> To-morrow, and to-morrow, and to-morrow
> Creeps in this petty pace from day to day
> To the last syllable of recorded time;
> And all our yesterdays have lighted fools
> The way to dusty death. Out, out, brief candle!
> Life's but a walking shadow, a poor player
> That struts and frets his hour upon the stage
> And then is heard no more. It is a tale
> Told by an idiot, full of sound and fury,
> Signifying nothing.   (V, v.)

And soon, in a speech as twisted with retrospective remorse, threats of hanging, and explosive violence as is this king:

[15]With Wilson Knight's "Macbeth at the last, by self-knowledge, gains grace" (*The Imperial Theme*, p. 128) I cannot agree; Macbeth gains, as we shall see, the knowledge of damnation, a knowledge the more horrid because wholly secular.

I gin to be aweary of the sun,
And wish th' estate o' th' world were now undone.
Ring the alarum-bell! Blow, wind! come, wrack!
At least we'll die with harness on our back.

(V, v.)

There speaks an aching weariness and a search for oblivion much in the manner of deformed Richard III. This awesome, throwback king of Scotland, furious and tender, putting his armor violently on and violently off during the greatest of Shakespeare's meditations, has, as he says, lived long enough. For he has known the infinite, and his soul is as dead as his wife.

Macbeth is Shakespeare's king, the ruler, the last prototype, a vision of barbarism aimed at in *Richard III* and *Henry V* but never reached until now—and reached now only when the poet, free of historical restrictions, could draw his own portrait of absolute power: a brutalizing, soul-wrenching reach for the ultimate and infinite, a bleak void in which, at last, even demonic evil for its own sake is lost in the swirl of violence.[16] The horror which is *Macbeth* is Shakespeare's great descent into the depths of the human soul, and the character Macbeth is simply raw force, as violent as evil. *Macbeth,* play and character, is the poet's last, scathing commentary upon the impulses that make men murderous because they are greedy. Macbeth is Shakespeare's greatest soldier, and, with Iago, his servant most devoid of human feeling.

Yet there is splendor in Macbeth; the emptiness of his soul is revealed in timeless, measured, reflective passages equaled in

[16]Wilson Knight's treatment of the major themes and images in *Macbeth* as kinds of ultimate polarities is at the end as persuasive as arbitrary: "In a final judgment the whole play may be writ down as a wrestling of destruction with creation: with sickening shocks the phantasmagoria of death and evil are violently loosed on earth, and for a while the agony endures, destructive; there is a wrenching of new birth, itself disorderly and unnatural, and then creation's more firm-set sequent concord replaces chaos. The baby-peace is crowned." (*The Imperial Theme,* p. 153.)

We wish at several points that Knight's treatment were less organic—as, for instance, when he discusses the theme of "honour," the word Iago used so badly and Falstaff, at Shrewsbury, so well.

their power only by his queen's sad half-sentences.[17] Their rhetorics, the king's and the queen's, are as opposite as their destinies; she, unimaginative and worldly to the tips of her bloodied fingers, is crushed and made mad by the very evils that enrich her husband's grandeur while impoverishing his soul.

For *Macbeth* is as much about imagination as about evil; as Macbeth's depravity deepens, his imagination broadens. It grows so great that it is able to encompass the full horror of the twisted creation he has become. Macbeth is autumn; his life is all theatrical shadow; his soul is too much charged with blood —yet he is the incarnation of imagination.

The process is familiar, for as Macbeth when we first meet him and when he becomes king is the personification of evil,[18] so gentle Bottom, in *A Midsummer Night's Dream,* was the personification of rustic stupidity. But Bottom, the ass's head off his shoulders, woke up: "the moment when Bottom awakens from this dream is the superb moment of the play. There is nothing more wonderful in the poet's early works and few things more wonderful in any of them. For what Shakespeare has caught here in perfection is the original miracle of the Imagination, the awakening of spiritual life in animal man."[19]

[17]Bradley on Lady Macbeth is Bradley at his finest, which is very fine indeed. "She never suspects that these deeds *must* be thought after these ways; that her facile realism, 'A little water clears us of this deed,' will one day be answered by herself, 'Will these hands ne'er be clean?' or that the fatal commonplace, 'What's done is done,' will make way for her last despairing sentence, 'What's done cannot be undone.' " (*Shakespearean Tragedy*, p. 298.)

[18]I disagree with Ribner's *a priori* assumptions about *Macbeth* as much as I admire the brilliance of his essay upon it; "Macbeth," he wrote, "is not like Richard a scourge of God whose evil course is a necessary element in a larger scheme"—a notion about which, in addition to my discussion of *Richard III* above, I would comment that the platitudinous Malcolm is of little more importance to us than was Fortinbras. Also, neither Fortinbras nor Malcolm—though Malcolm is a prig—offends, as does Henry Tudor. Ribner feels that Macbeth is "like Othello, a man of potential goodness" (*Patterns*, p. 154); it is necessary to observe that such initial reporting as we have of Othello's martial behavior is Desdemona's. The martial Macbeth is by contrast rendered to us through the medium of the captain's horrid images in *Macbeth* I, ii.

[19]Goddard, p. 80.

In *Macbeth* Shakespeare catches again the same miracle—the birth of imagination. And in *Macbeth* it is a mighty miracle indeed; the rustic Bottom wakens to new life, but Macbeth, spiritually rotted, awakens to death. The king is not, like Bottom, gross matter redeemed, nor like Hamlet the burial of imagination in self-consuming thought; he is the savage awakening both to the conception of soul and to the lack of soul in himself. Macbeth at last is supremely tragic because he is aware—fully aware—of what he has done and of its meaninglessness in that cosmos which he has defied. He dies in a wealth of self-realization—which his violence to messengers casts away for a moment, but does not deny—and his death is as grand as his life was futile. His awareness is as complete as was his communion with barbarism, and he is as transfigured by imagination as he was disfigured by evil. But his transfiguration brings him only to what his deeds have made him deserve: a vision of irremediable futility, a stark void where remorse may not live and where reason dares not dwell.

This last vision of Macbeth is ugly indeed. In it Macbeth's creator has provided, for all time, a view of the abysses of tyranny—and an explanation of its endless fascination. But no century has known better than our own that a lesson writ in blood is not necessarily a lesson learned. And perhaps no century has been less prepared than our own to accept the transcendent miracle of transfiguration that is *King Lear*.

There is no more eloquent testimony to the severity of perfect justice, which is the operative principle of *King Lear,* than the survival for a century and a half of Nahum Tate's altered version.[20] Inexorable justice, intolerably harsh because so personalized and so centered in the figure of the aged king, is the theme of the play. And justice in this sense is moral law; Goneril, Regan, and Edmund, dead, are the fulfillment of Albany's "Humanity must perforce prey on itself,/ Like monsters of the deep." (IV, ii.) Yet Albany has asked that the heavens send visible spirits to redeem humanity: ". . . the heavens did—and King Lear did not fail them.

[20]Bradley records that "Betterton acted Tate's version; Garrick acted it and Dr. Johnson approved it." (*Shakespearean Tragedy,* p. 197.)

> You are a spirit, I know; where did you die? . . .
>
> (*King Lear*, IV, vii.)

> Do you see this? Look on her, look, her lips,
> Look there, look there!
>
> (*King Lear*, V, iii.)

And so, in *King Lear* at least, humanity did not devour itself, and King Lear and his child were lifted up into the realm of the gods."[21]

It is not necessary, in order to perceive that Lear's last moments form a wonder of redemption, to join Goddard and Bradley in their insistence that Lear at last feels not grief but joy.[22] It is sufficient for our purpose to recognize that Lear dies a man transformed, made over by suffering in the way Aeschylus so long ago described:

> Zeus, who guided men to think,
> Who has laid it down that wisdom
> Alone comes through suffering.
> Still there drips in sleeping against the heart
> Grief of memory; against
> Our pleasure we are temperate.
> From the gods who sit in grandeur
> Grace comes somehow violent.
>
> (*Agamemnon*, 176–83.)

---

[21]Goddard, p. 556.

[22]Bradley noticed the most important of the many parallels between Lear and Gloucester; surely Edgar's recounting of his father's death—"his flaw'd heart . . . / Twixt two extremes of passion, joy and grief,/ Burst smilingly." (V, iii.)—strengthens Bradley's contention that the actor who plays Lear "is false to the text who does not attempt to express, in Lear's last accents and gestures and look, an unbearable joy." (*Shakespearean Tragedy*, p. 234.) Theodore Spencer quotes Bradley's injunction to the actor and extends its implications: "In his [Lear's] own mind she [Cordelia] lives; and it is the discovery that Cordelia is alive, that life is the reality under the appearance, that the reality is *good*—it is this that breaks his heart." (*Shakespeare*, p. 152.) Ribner describes Lear's death as a "moment of insupportable ecstasy" (*Patterns*, p. 122), and Goddard, writing also of Lear's last speech, asks, "Why but to make the old king's dying assertion incontrovertible does Shakespeare so permeate his play with the theme of vision?" (*The Meaning of Shakespeare*, p. 549.)

The grace that illuminates *King Lear* is indeed violent. Gloucester is blinded, but "I have no way," he tells his cruelly used
son, "and therefore want no eyes;/ I stumbled when I saw."
(IV, i.) Lear, the storm's rage matched by his own, is exposed
upon the heath; yet:

> In, boy; go first. You houseless poverty,—
> Nay, get thee in. I'll pray, and then I'll sleep.
> Poor naked wretches, wheresoe'er you are,
> That bide the pelting of this pitiless storm,
> How shall your houseless heads and unfed sides,
> Your loop'd and window'd raggedness, defend you
> From seasons such as these? O, I have ta'en
> Too little care of this! Take physic, pomp;
> Expose thyself to feel what wretches feel,
> That thou mayst shake the superflux to them,
> And show the heavens more just.   (III, iv.)

There is much mercy, if little egalitarianism, in this, and Lear's
identification with the outcast lends irony to his confrontation
with Kent:

> Kent: How fares your Grace?
> Lear: What's he?   (III, iv.)

That is surely not Lear's request for identification of the earl,
but rather an acceptance on Lear's part of the absence of the
regality which so corrupted him.

For corrupt he was. After her father's dispersal of his kingdom, Regan observes, and accurately, that Lear "hath ever but
slenderly known himself." (I, i.) And this—the gaining of
self-knowledge by the self-deposed king—is the dramatic process
of *King Lear*. His self-knowledge is won among hardships un-
imaginable, and is forged in the crucible of madness. But it is
achieved.

The king's sufferings on the heath are matched only by
his vanity and consequent folly; yet as the king dispenses his
kingdom among his daughters there is a kind of love in him,
however perverted. Cordelia is his favorite and she shall have
the greatest share—and the king will sport with a hundred

gentlemen. But it all, the greatest cameo-scene Shakespeare ever
wrote, depends upon words—words, and Lear's understanding
of them. That Goneril and Regan are false he has recognized
at least enough to prefer Cordelia to them, yet Cordelia's brave,
defiant "I love your Majesty/ According to my bond; no more,
no less" (I, i) expresses a love too rightly in proportion for
the king to understand.

As king, so earl: Gloucester's rude, careless introduction of
Edmund to Kent is no more forgivable than is the king's vain
misappraisal of his daughters: "Though this knave came something saucily to the world before he was sent for, yet was his
mother fair; there was good sport at his making, and the
whoreson must be acknowledged." (I, i.) They are of an age,
the king and the Earl of Gloucester—careless, crude, grown old
and blind in their place and power; they, taken apart or taken
together, are Shakespeare's comment upon public men. For
Lear's first public act in the play—the giving away of his function with his kingdom—is an act of monumental vanity, and
the earl's crudity with his illegitimate son is no more than the
coarseness of the public man transferred to the private sphere.
The two are as foolish as old, and it is the Fool who, when
taking Lear's measure, measures them both: "Thou shouldst
not have been old till thou hadst been wise." (I, v.) Gloucester
is no more a man—in Macbeth's sense—than is Lear, and
neither is more a man than Richard II, the king of shadows:

> LEAR: Doth any here know me? This is not Lear.
> Doth Lear walk thus? Speak thus? Where
>   are his eyes?
> Either his notion weakens, his discernings
> Are lethargied—Ha! waking? 'Tis not so.
> Who is it that can tell who I am?
> FOOL: Lear's shadow.   (I, iv.)

It is not in palaces that Lear finds himself, but in hovels,
on heaths and fields. He learns pity as he feels what wretches
feel. In the frenzy of madness, he is met by Gloucester—a confrontation of ruinations, each matching complementary sorrows,
each craving a sort of reconciliation with the brutal world of

which once they were masters, through the medium of pity for each other. To Gloucester's anguished, "O, let me kiss that hand!" Lear replies, "Let me wipe it first; it smells of mortality." (IV, vi.) The erstwhile king dispenses chaotic justice to the adulterer, uttering the most memorable of Shakespeare's strictures against public men and their Commodity:

> Plate sins with gold,
> And the strong lance of justice hurtless
> breaks;
> Arm it in rags, a pigmy's straw does
> pierce it . . .
> Get thee glass eyes,
> And, like a scurvy politician, seem
> To see the things thou dost not.
> (IV, vi.)

A severe indictment—but not applied to himself by the erstwhile king who has yet to learn that his power no longer is equal to his rage: ". . . kill, kill, kill, kill, kill, kill!"

Pity of self may be the medium of pity for others. The earl, blinded, sent to "smell his way to Dover" (III, vii), passes from the despair of "As flies to wanton boys, are we to the Gods/ They kill us for their sport" (IV, i) to a moment of magnificent resignation:

> Henceforth I'll bear
> Affliction till it do cry out itself
> "Enough, enough" and die.
> (IV, vi.)

And Lear, ". . . come to this great stage of fools" (IV, vi) must lose all to gain all. Rescued by Cordelia and from madness, he is, upon wakening, superbly pitiable:

> Pray, do not mock me.
> I am a very foolish fond old man,
> Fourscore and upward, not an hour more or less;
> And, to deal plainly,
> I fear I am not in my perfect mind.
> Methinks I should know you, and know this man;

> Yet I am doubtful; for I am mainly ignorant
> What place this is, and all the skill I have
> Remembers not these garments; nor I know not
> Where I did lodge last night. Do not laugh at me;
> For, as I am a man, I think this lady
> To be my child Cordelia.   (IV, vii.)

Lear is Shakespeare's only king who forgets the purpose of his robes but can recognize his child. Having been among beggars of late, he has learned to beg a little himself: "Pray you now, forget and forgive; I am old and foolish." (IV, vii) Lear is careless of defeat, for he no longer cares for the world; his rage and ferocity are replaced by a love no longer perverted and still rightly placed; he has lost a kingdom and regained himself:

> Come, let's away to prison;
> We two alone will sing like birds i' the' cage.
> When thou dost ask me blessing, I'll kneel down
> And ask of thee forgiveness. So we'll live,
> And pray, and sing, and tell old tales, and laugh
> At gilded butterflies, and hear poor rogues
> Talk of court news; and we'll talk with them too,
> Who loses and who wins; who's in, who's out;
> And take upon 's the mystery of things
> As if we were God's spies; and we'll wear out,
> In a wall'd prison, packs and sects of great ones,
> That ebb and flow by th' moon.   (V, ii.)

Shakespeare never wrote any poetry better than that because none of his characters had anything as fine as that to say. It is his most sublime irony that none of his kings—not Henry V at Agincourt nor Macbeth in the perfection of his communion with evil—ever envisions for himself as grand a destiny as does Lear. Richard II's prison contained a world; Lear's prison is the world. And Lear, unlike Richard, is the world's observer. When Bottom and imagination were reborn together, Bottom wakened to the world; but when Lear's imagination casts about it for reality, it finds the world within Lear himself—to be shared with the daughter whom now, because he has found his world, he truly loves.[23]

But realization of his vision is denied him. He who has renounced love will have love torn from him—just as in Macbeth we saw that the man who embraces the world will find his arms horribly empty. Lear's daughter and his Fool are dead,[24] and in a last, supreme moment of brutal irony the crown which he had so abused is placed, by well-meaning Albany, back upon his aged head. But Lear is in spirit with his Fool and his daughter; he does not hear Albany; death is upon him.

The unspeakable cruelty of Lear's being made king again is supportable only because Lear has had his vision. And as Lear's vision of imprisonment with his daughter is Shakespeare's greatest poetic moment, so also this vision—the birth of imagination in a good old man, once king, once mad, and for a time mad and king together—marks the high point of Shakespeare's rulers: Lear wishes to observe the world, not to rule it, and to be alone with the child he loves. He would tell stories, as old men will, but no lies, as old kings do.

[23]"*Henry V* is an account of how a man became a king. *King Lear* is an account of how a king became a man. Until you have read *King Lear,* you have not read *Henry V.*" (Goddard, p. 527.) Surely Goddard here has reached not only Shakespeare's "meaning" but his spirit. There is a sense in which *King Lear* is Shakespeare's most political play: nowhere else in Shakespeare is either the need for order among men or the ravages of power upon those who must provide order more pitilessly revealed.

[24]Ribner wrote in 1960 that "in Lear's final 'And my poor fool is hang'd' (V. iii. 305), which obviously refers to Cordelia, we are told also of the fate of the Fool, for it appears that both parts were played by the same boy actor, and we can assume that the Jacobean audience would have recognized in Lear's arms the body not only of his redeeming daughter, but that of his redeeming fool as well." (*Patterns,* p. 136.) While I think that this reading of the line—earlier advanced, Kenneth Muir tells us, by Sir Arthur Quiller-Couch and others—is a most happy mean between extremes, Muir regards it as conclusively refuted. (See his notes in the Arden *King Lear,* p. 217.) And G. I. Guthrie, who edited the new Cambridge *King Lear* under the supervision of Dover Wilson, noted (p. 274) that "surely the Fool, like Kent, is forgotten."

I cannot believe that the limitations of Shakespeare's stage were such as to demand of the poet that his greatest king forget the Fool, who was in the days of Lear's horror both his tormentor and the redemptive focus of his love.

Much has been written, and more will be, about ideal kings and ideal relationships in Shakespeare. We have found no ideal kings. Lear, ripened by years, is nearly crazed with vanity, and must cease to be a king of men before he becomes, to Goddard, not ". . . Nature's king, but Heaven's."[25] And the picture of Lear, regal in his rags, no longer king of men but soon to be king of self, recalls another portrayal of tired majesty: Henry VI at Towton, king only of his molehill, giving over to God the issue of a battle which concerns his throne but not himself: ". . . Methinks it were a happy life/ To be no better than a homely swain." (*3 Henry VI*, II, iv.) So is dismissed the agony and hollow glory of Agincourt.

But there are ideal relationships in Shakespeare, because there are great men. Lear, though hugely perverted by years and position, is a man of great dimensions when we meet him, and those dimensions broaden as his worldly pretensions shrink. The ideal relationship is not political, but personal; the Earl of Kent, the Fool, and Cordelia all begin and remain within that relationship to the great individual which, to Shakespeare, must have constituted the ideal. But the full strength of this relationship is manifested only as Lear himself, brought by the vicissitudes of his life from spiritual blindness to inner sight, first perceives dimly, "Mine eyes are not o' th' best," and at last clearly, "I'll see that straight." (V, iii.) And at the end Lear sees Kent as straight as he has, with Cordelia, seen the world; he may mourn his Fool and his daughter, but his vision—not his crown—is the fulfillment of his life.

[25]*The Meaning of Shakespeare,* p. 535.

IX ❧ Parable Turned Paradox: The Garden Revisited

WE have earlier observed that civil philosophy at its highest is moral philosophy; the greatest, then, of the Shakespearean exercises is that the demonology explicated by and among his English kings culminated in the cosmology which is *King Lear*. And it is good to know that the poet who became wealthy as he progressively succeeded in refining art from the brutal crudities of history also grew wise in the process. But we must, as we conclude our study, remember that one does not construct retrospective orthodoxies about flagging, and at best fragile, institutions; it is given only to the few—and those few who like Macaulay were, or are, party men first and students of history second—to become doctrinaire. The genteel cynicism which marked and marred the great work of Edward Gibbon is the historian's most becoming pose.

If, as legend has it, Shakespeare died as gloriously full of food and drink as his Falstaff had lived, we neglect the ironies of history unless we remember that in the year Shakespeare died Oliver Cromwell, then seventeen, was a year older than the century he was to dominate. Not long, as years count in history, did the monarchy which Shakespeare considered with such perception outlive him. As the head of Charles I fell from his shoulders, so fell the form of monarchy which has been the subject of this, and Shakespeare's work. That the final frantic attempt at despotism made by Strafford and Laud and their king was of such short duration so soon after Shakespeare's death simply demonstrates the exactitude of the poet's impalatable Allegory of the Garden in *Richard II*.

Despotism may be detestable—as Shakespeare found it through his presentation of Henry IV, who bloodied his own kingdom, and Henry V, who bloodied his kingdom too by using his people to bloody the kingdom of others—but despotism must be, as Shakespeare and Machiavelli recognized, both thorough and remorseless even to survive, let alone succeed. Dante no less than Machiavelli was willing to sacrifice the moral nature of the ruler for the unity of the kingdom, and regarded such sacrifice as the burden of rule.[1] The instincts of Dante and Machiavelli were essentially conservative, as were the instincts of Shakespeare, who, after all, read Lancastrian-oriented, Tudor-bought party histories and preferred the House of York. Shakespeare—however much he, litigious and greedy, loved the city which was not long after his death to approve, in an act of singular ill wisdom and monumental bad taste, the rule of Oliver Cromwell—was, like his Richard III, a man bred of the provinces and not of the city. Shakespeare chose—as the historical Richard III ought to have chosen to remain at York had not ambition and his brother's people called him to London—to finish out his life in the town where he was born and his father was disgraced, doubtless to the immense, and much relished, discomfiture of his elder neighbors.

So we may presume that Shakespeare, like most men who aspire to become rich or wise or both, was early captured by the immensely rewarding record of his countrymen's atrocious behavior toward each other—such behavior being, after all, the substance both of history and of that peculiar form of melodrama which the history, or chronicle, play represents. He

[1]It is interesting in this connection that Dante, possibly ill at ease over his own audacity, put Curio, who was supposed by Lucan to have advised his wavering general to cross the Rubicon, among the Sowers of Discord. Curio's general, however, despite his singular lack of virtue, reposes himself, in Dante's cosmology, among the Virtuous Pagans, while his murderers are gnawed in two of Satan's three mouths. (See Canto IV, and Dorothy Sayers' note, pp. 315–16.)

wrote within obvious limitations; for instance, Henry Tudor, no matter how one may feel about his secretive, covetous reign, did in point of fact win the battle of Market Bosworth and succeeded, despite his singular unpopularity, in keeping his uneasy seat. The manly exertions of Henry VIII, of whom Bindoff observes that "the reputed boast of Henry's old age, that he had never spared a woman in his lust, was perhaps as far from the truth as its demonstrably false counterpart, that he had never spared a man in his anger,"[2] gave to his country, by way of progeny, two disasters and a miracle. At Elizabeth's accession it took no great age to remember the minority of Edward and the excesses of Mary and Cardinal Pole; neither did it take, as Elizabeth grew old and the great poet of her reign ripened to his maturity, a political philosopher to recognize that a kingdom without an heir is mortally ill. And, just as Henry VII had, whether he would or no, to execute the Earl of Warwick, so Elizabeth had to ennoble a judge and temporarily disgrace her secretary while she railed against—or pretended to rail against—her council's overhasty handling of the writ of execution delivered against the mother of the Stuarts.

But Elizabeth the Queen—herself no mean student, either of statecraft, her own uneasy line, or the drama—was another of the limitations placed around Shakespeare. He was restrained by the facts of history known to his audiences, the myths, whether true or false, which they had been taught, and the will of a tempestuous, rather wicked queen who saw, or thought she saw, or pretended to see, herself in Shakespeare's dangerous, as it proved in the event, rendering of the reign of Richard II. So, as Shakespeare set himself to the dramatization of English history, he was as beset by restrictions as he was rich in opportunities. For it is not least among the grandeurs of medieval society that from its squalor and injustice there emerge titanic, satanic, figures. Upon those figures Shakespeare, with his sure eye for the sensational, seized with the surety of the dramatist born to the trade.

It is well for men who wish to understand civil order to study anarchy, and it was within the chaotic hell which was

[2]*Tudor England,* p. 69.

the historical Henry V's legacy to England that Shakespeare found his first great characters. It is no historical accident that the rule of the weak gives reign to upstarts, and the pious, sick Henry VI was no better a match for his nobles than were his father's generals for Joan of Arc. But within Shakespeare's first trilogy patterns early develop: the French witch's place is taken in the ruination of England's affairs by the French trollop-queen Margaret; it is she, not the king, who is a match for the king's treacherous, brawling nobles.

The problems of the first trilogy are solved in *Richard III,* the play that has stood in the history of the theater so wholly alone because it is so remarkably playable. Richard III resolves the problems of his kingdom by the simplest of methods— execution—and although his bloody reign is difficult to approve, in history or in drama, it is as easy to justify his murders in political terms as it is impossible—save for those entirely devoid of humor or irony—not to relish his sardonic amusement at the purposes and effects of his own acting. The citizen's line, "Woe to the land that's govern'd by a child!" (*Richard III,* II, iii) must have rung through Shakespeare's theater like an echoing bell, recalling vividly the disasters of the child Edward's reign. But the audience, happily, could not have known that the line of Lords Protector was not too long hence to be extended by another ominous Protector—who, with his major-generals, paved the way for England's greatest king, Charles II, to cure the nation, with his wit, wisdom, and mistresses, of Puritanism and its attendant ills as thoroughly as any man could.

Perhaps the most remarkable feature of *Richard III* is that, at the end, the murderous king, isolated at Market Bosworth against Henry Tudor and the foreign scum and domestic traitors who put him on the throne, is both magnificently alone and magnificently English; the Tudor will become king, but Richard becomes the Knight who has purged England of Henry V's pernicious legacy. To Henry Tudor, who, after all, was the grandfather of the reigning queen, goes the battle—but the play, like its predecessors, goes to Richard and York. As Palmer observed, Richard does not become a monster until he loses his father the duke; Richard the monster does not become human again until, crying for a horse so that he may fight, he becomes like his father—the brawling, contentious, but conscience-hampered Knight whom order must supress but whom all men admire.

Then Shakespeare, his grasp of historical compression assured and, perhaps, his interest in the causes of anarchy quickened by the four plays in which he had presented the effects of anarchy, went back in time. We group *King John* and *Richard II* together because, in terms of theme and substance, they share so much. The modern historian vilifies John by exalting—far beyond its worth—the Charter unearthed by the seventeenth-century parliamentarian who paved the way for Lord Oliver's Saints; Shakespeare and the historians of his generation disliked the first and only John to rule England not because necessity made him capitulate at Runnymede but because John, to rescue himself from his barons, held his crown not from his people but from his pope. Within the Plantagenet John, there lay a hell; within another Plantagenet, John of Gaunt, the Duke of Lancaster whose son was shortly to succeed his nephew, there also lay a hell. For John of Gaunt's nephew, the second Richard to rule England, had, as surely as John, leased out his kingdom—and not in order to rule, but to reign, extravagantly.

So both John and Richard were weak, bad men, and while the succession in *King John* is assured through the exercises of Faulconbridge and destroyed in *Richard II* by the crafty, cold treachery of Henry Bolingbroke, the lesson from the two is plain: kings could be conquered and destroyed by either of the props—the church or the nobles—which should sustain them. From the deficiencies of John and Richard, Shakespeare drew a savage moral that became the guiding principle of the exercise in demonology contained in the two parts of *Henry IV* and *Henry V*. To repeat that moral as it appears in *Richard II*: "Go," the Gardener tells his assistants,

> bind thou up yon dangling apricocks,
> Which, like unruly children, make their sire
> Stoop with oppression of their prodigal weight;

Give some supportance to the bending twigs.
Go thou, and like an executioner,
Cut off the heads of too fast-growing sprays
That look too lofty in our commonwealth;
All must be even in our government.

(III, iv.)

The allegory of the old Gardener and his grim, efficient assistants is Shakespeare's only intrusive borrowing from the methodology of the old Morality. And the principles of the allegory are quickly to be applied: Henry Bolingbroke will decorate London with the heads of his adversaries because he must—though he protests—bathe himself in blood if he is to rule. The fault of Richard II, who kept the Garden of State badly, becomes the grisly virtue of Henry IV: all will be even in his commonwealth—even, or dead. It is a grim polity, and Henry IV, like his son before Agincourt, Richard III, and later Macbeth, does not sleep, until his last and permanent sleep in the Jerusalem chamber of his palace. As Socrates, another wicked aristrocrat, if not by breeding then by taste and temperament, said to his jury: "I suppose that if anyone were told to pick out the night on which he slept so soundly as not even to dream, and then to compare it with all the other nights and days of his life, and then were told to say, after due consideration, how many better and happier days and nights than this he had spent in the course of his life—well, I think that even the Gerat King himself, to say nothing of any private person, would find these days and nights easy to count in comparison with the rest."[3] And Henry V, who took with ferocious eagerness his father's last advice—"busy giddy minds/ With foreign quarrels"—does not sleep before Agincourt.

"I am afeard," the soldier Williams tells his disguised monarch, on the eve of Agincourt, "there are few die well that die in a battle." (*Henry V*, IV, i.) And, as we have seen, the ferocity of Harry of Monmouth's rhetoric, his slaughter of his prisoners, say as eloquently as had his father, that "rage and hot blood are his counsellors." If, as some of Shakespeare's

[3]Plato, p. 75.

readers have supposed, Henry V is either the ideal king or the servant of God, he ought then to have ruled Sparta, or to have served that Mars whose temple's gates Virgil hoped, with his Imperial master, would, after Actium, be forever closed. No less an animal than Macbeth but unlike Macbeth an animal without fruition, Henry V is the spirit of war—as savage as rapacious.

If, as the aphorism has it, politics is the art of the possible, it is no less true that a remarkable number of great students of government who were also great artists have turned from fact to illusion, or at least to an idealization of the real. Plato thought that if men were wise, they would also be virtuous; so in the *Republic* he specified how men might be made wise, and in his judgment fit to rule. But in the *Laws* we discover, as the Athenian promulgates the last of Plato's ideal polities, how easy and how brief is the short step from beneficent despotism to the tyranny of the arrogant aristocrat. Virgil celebrated the peace of Augustus because he was paid to do so, and might even have believed in it. Virgil's most astute pupil, Dante, in another time, place, and war, came to regard the church and the state as coordinate, and together divinely ordained. Seizing upon the happy accident of the short span of years between the birth of Julius Caesar and the birth of Jesus, Dante as he grew older amid chaos came to believe that a universal state which had goodness as its object and a purified church which had salvation as its object would function as mutual correctives— an idea that—despite its patent idealism, seems the most astute answer to the problems—nationalism and ecclesiastical greed— of medieval society as Dante knew it.

Thus it is one of the striking curiosities of human thought that the greatest of the Greek poets after Homer, the greatest of the Roman court poets, and the foremost citizen of Florence all settled upon a form of tyranny less harsh because less realistic than that of Shakespeare's Gardener in *Richard II*.

It is of course the presence of Falstaff, and the dismal story of the degeneration of his relationship with his hypocritical prince, which render the two parts of *Henry IV* dramatic. We may move with relish from tavern to court and back again, for the tavern is the home of those happy misdemeanors beloved by all save the most puritanical. The court, as we have noticed, is the home of the felonies which the joy of the tavern makes appear empty, though realistic. It is with the invention of Falstaff that we sense the poet's growing disinterest in the doctrinaire. Shakespeare has given us the Gardener; in *Henry IV* he has given us the Gardener's king; and in Henry V he has shown us how the Gardener's doctrine works out in human hands: civil control lapsing into savagery. The distance between Henry IV and his son is perhaps best measured by recalling the difference between Plato's *Republic* and his *Laws,* or between Dante the character and Filippo Argenti, Dante's personification of purposeless wrath.

So Shakespeare had done with real kings, and with the houses of Lancaster and York. He came to consider not the nature of nations but the nature of men. He wrote, in *Hamlet* and *Julius Caesar,* about men remote in time and place; he wrote, not of the tragedies of nations, but of the personal tragedies arising from intellection and from unthinking, undiscriminating acceptance of ancestral ways and precepts. Both Brutus and Hamlet are grave, reflective men who pause not to think but to brood. The brooding of Marcus Brutus leads him to murder not what is but what might be; the brooding of Hamlet leads to nothing but further brooding. Both Brutus and Hamlet are victims of that uncritical fidelity to outworn tradition which the poet excoriates.

In his last two studies of British kings, Shakespeare, unhampered by restrictions of factual material and personal danger, wrought a vision first of hell and then of heaven. The ethical center shifted, as he moved from the chronicle play to tragedy, from the body politic to the unique conditions of two great men . One of them, Macbeth, had to give all to gain what was, at last, horridly but grandly nothing; the other, King Lear, had to give all and suffer much to discover what, in the whole world which had once been his, he could love. It is among the human tragedies that the lesson Shakespeare taught must be learned, and that usually too late, by men in their individual capacities. The poet must have wished us to believe, or perhaps to hope, that love is a greater thing even than power. Assuredly Shakespeare had come to know, as Machiavelli taught, that to be royal is to be alone, to be cut off from ordinary human ties—and that such estrangement breeds, as it did in Richard III, Henry V, and finally Macbeth, the capacity for ultimate atrocity.

Bibliography of Sources

I owe much to the many editors of Shakespeare's plays upon whose work I have depended. I relied most heavily upon the dating done by Charles Sisson, used the standard American edition of the complete plays and poems prepared by Professors Neilson and Hill, and consulted with great frequency the New Cambridge and Arden prefaces, notes, and texts. For the convenience of the reader I have chosen not to enumerate all the sources I consulted in the preparation of this book; I list below only those from which I quoted or to which I referred in the text.

Aeschylus. *The Agamemnon.* Translated and edited by Richmond Lattimore. In volume I of *The Complete Greek Tragedies,* edited by David Greene and Richmond Lattimore. Chicago: University of Chicago Press, 1964.

Anonymous. *Woodstock: A Moral History.* Edited by A. P. Rossiter. London: Chatto and Windus, 1946.

Bindoff, S.T. *Tudor England.* Harmondsworth, Middlesex: Penguin Books, 1959.

Boklund, Gunnar. "Judgment in *Hamlet.*" In *Essays on Shakespeare,* edited by Gerald Chapman. Princeton: Princeton University Press, 1965.

Bradley, A.C. *Shakespearean Tragedy.* New York: Meridian Press, 1959.

Brockbank, J.P. "The Frame of Disorder—*Henry VI.*" In *Shakespeare: The Histories,* edited by Eugene M. Wraith. Englewood Cliffs, New Jersey: Prentice Hall, 1965.

Campbell, Lily B. *Shakespeare's Tragic Heroes: Slaves of Passion.* New York: Barnes and Noble, 1966.

Dante Aleghieri. *The Comedy of Dante Aleghieri, the Florentine: Cantica I.,* translated by Dorothy L. Sayers. Edinburgh: Penguin Press, 1950.

Eliot, T.S. "Tradition and the Individual Talent." In *Essays in English,* edited by Paul C. Wermuth. New York: Holt, Rinehart, Winston, 1967.

Erikson, Eric H. *Young Man Luther: A Study in Psychoanalysis and History.* New York: Norton and Co., 1962.

Fabyan, Robert. *The New Chronicles of England and France.* Excerpted in volume IV of *Narrative and Dramatic Sources of Shakespeare,* edited by Geoffrey Bullough. New York: Columbia University Press, 1960.

Foxe, John. *Actes and Monuments of Martrys.* Excerpted in volume III of *Narrative and Dramatic Sources of Shakespeare,* edited by Geoffrey Bullough. New York: Columbia University Press, 1960.

Goddard, Harold. *The Meaning of Shakespeare.* Chicago: University of Chicago Press, 1951.

Hall, Edward. *The Union of the Two Noble and Illustre Families of Lancastre and Yorke.* Excerpted in volumes III and IV of *Narrative and Dramatic Sources of Shakespeare,* edited by Geoffrey Bullough. New York: Columbia University Press, 1960.

Holinshed, Raphaell. *The Third Volume of Chronicles.* Excerpted in volume IV of *Narrative and Dramatic Sources of Shakespeare,* edited by Geoffrey Bullough. New York: Columbia University Press, 1960.

Kendall, Paul Murray. *Richard the Third.* Garden City, New York: Doubleday and Co., 1965.

Knight, G. Wilson. *The Imperial Theme: Further Interpretations of Shakespeare's Tragedies, including the Roman Plays.* London: University Paperbacks, 1965.

————. *The Sovereign Flower.* London: Methuen and Co., 1958.

Knights, L.C. *Further Explorations.* Stanford, California: Stanford University Press, 1965.

Lewis, Wyndham. *The Lion and the Fox: The Role of the Hero in the Plays of Shakespeare.* London: Barnes and Noble, n.d.

Machiavelli, Niccolo. *The Prince.* Translated by Luigi Ricci. New York: New American Library, 1953.

Neale, J.E. *Queen Elizabeth I*. London: J. Cape, 1959.

Palmer, John. *Political and Comic Characters of Shakespeare*. London: Macmillan and Co., 1962.

Plato. *The Apology*. Translated by Hugh Tredennick. In *The Last Days of Socrates*, edited by Betty Radice and Robert Baldich. London: Penguin Books, 1965.

Reese, M.M. *The Cease of Majesty: A Study of Shakespeare's History Plays*. New York, St. Martin's Press, 1961.

————. *Shakespeare: His World and His Work*. London: Edward Arnold, 1964.

Ribner, Irving. *The English History Play in the Age of Shakespeare*. Princeton: Princeton University Press, 1957. Revised edition (London: Methuen and Co.), 1965.

————. *Patterns in Shakespearean Tragedy*. London: Methuen and Co., 1964.

Richmond, H.M. *Shakespeare: Political Plays*. New York: Random House, 1967.

Rossiter, A.P. "Angel with Horns: The Unity of *Richard III*." In *Shakespeare: The Histories*, edited by Eugene M. Wraith. Englewood Cliffs, New Jersey: Prentice Hall, 1965.

Shakespeare, William. *Macbeth*. Edited by Kenneth Muir. London: Methuen and Co., 1959.

————. *King Lear*. Edited by Kenneth Muir. London: Methuen and Co., 1959.

————. *The Complete Plays and Poems of William Shakespeare*. Edited by William Allan Neilson and Charles Jarvis Hill. Cambridge, Massachusetts: Riverside Press, 1942.

————. *The Complete Works of Shakespeare*. Edited by Charles Jasper Sisson. New York: Harper and Bros., 1960.

————. *King Henry V and Macbeth*. Edited by J. H. Walter. London: Methuen and Co., 1954.

————. *Julius Caesar*. Edited by J. Dover Wilson. Cambridge, England: Cambridge University Press, 1956.

————. *Henry V*. Edited by J. Dover Wilson. Cambridge, England: Cambridge University Press, 1955.

————. *Macbeth*. Edited by J. Dover Wilson. Cambridge, England: Cambridge University Press, 1960.

————. *King Lear*. Edited by J. Dover Wilson and G. I. Guthrie. Cambridge, England: Cambridge University Press, 1960.

Spencer, Theodore. *Shakespeare and the Nature of Man.* (Lowell Lectures, 1942.) New York: Macmillan Co., 1955.

Tillyard, E.M.W. *Shakespeare's History Plays.* New York: Barnes and Noble, 1964.

Traversi, D.A. *An Approach to Shakespeare.* 3rd edition, revised. Garden City, New York: Doubleday and Co., 1969.

————. *Shakespeare: From Richard II to Henry V.* Stanford, California: Stanford University Press, 1961.

Trevelyan, George M. *History of England.* 2 vols. Garden City, New York: Doubleday and Co., 1952.

Van Doren, Mark. *Shakespeare.* Garden City, New York: Henry Holt Co., 1939.

Wilson, J. Dover. *The Fortunes of Falstaff.* (Clark Lectures, 1943.) New York: Macmillan Co., 1945.

————. *What Happens in Hamlet.* Cambridge, England: Cambridge University Press, 1959.

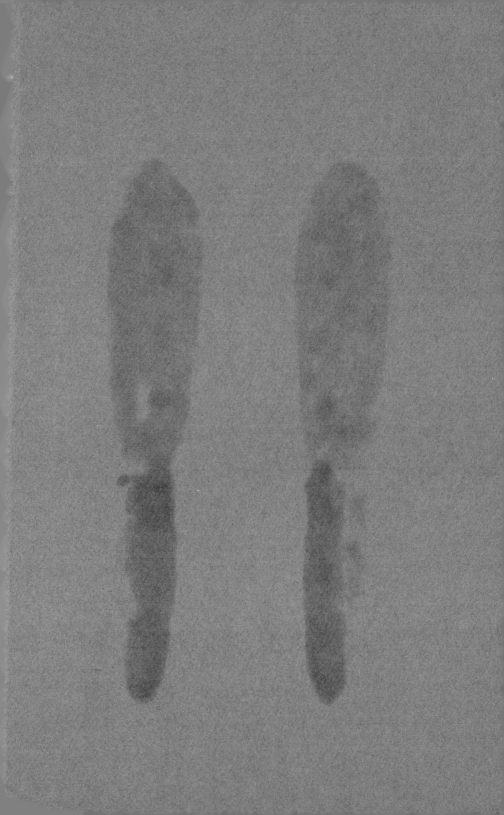

70829

PR
2982
B7

BROMLEY, JOHN
    THE SHAKESPEAREAN KINGS.

DATE DUE

DATE DUE	
DEC 14 2000	
DEC 1 1 2006	

Fernald Library
Colby-Sawyer College
New London, New Hampshire

GAYLORD   PRINTED IN U.S.A.